AYAHUASCA

Soul Medicine of the Amazon Jungle

Expanded second edition, 2017

JAVIER REGUEIRO

A Comprehensive and Practical Guide

For Don Francisco Montes Shuña, my teacher,
Joseph Kramer, weaver of magic, and
Ken S., elder extraordinaire

Invocation to the Mother

Oh won't you come into me
And flow like a river through me
Over me
Around me
Slipping around my stones
Tumbling over my waterfalls
Uncovering the hidden treasures
Known only in my heart of hearts
Trickling, seeping towards my golden Center.
Allowing me
Encouraging me
Teaching me
How to truly unfold
Like a flower
Naturally, unselfconsciously
Like the heart beat of time
Pulsing through me.
I think I may know it
Like a mantra
Woven into my memory
But oh, to repeat these precious steps
To walk the labyrinth of this life
To remember my soul's desire.
As I feel the earth beneath my feet
And the Mother's tender loving
I know that I have chosen well,
I have floated upon
This pond
Before.
And reflected myself towards
The same sky.

I have stumbled
I have wondered
I still wonder...
But with each drop of knowing
My thirst becomes less
I allow trust to mingle with my heart
I see the brave and beautiful dance
That we all dance
And I fall back on these tender ancient bones of the
Mother
And embrace this golden life.

Erin McAuley, Pisac, May 2009

Our deepest fear is not that we are inadequate. Our deepest fear is that we are powerful beyond measure. It is our light, not our darkness, that most frightens us.
We ask ourselves "Who am I to be brilliant, gorgeous, talented and fabulous?"
Actually, who are you not to be?
You are a child of God. Your playing small doesn't serve the world. There is nothing enlightened about shrinking so that other people won't feel insecure around you.
We are born to make manifest the Glory of God that is within us. It's not just in some of us, it's in everyone.
And as we let our own light shine, we unconsciously give other people permission to do the same.
As we are liberated from our own fear, our presence automatically liberates others.

Marianne Williamson[1]

---

1   Williamson, Marianne. *A Return To Love*. New York, HarperOne, 1992.

CONTENTS

CONTENTS

Part I

"Uku Pacha" by Harry Chavez, 2010

FORWORD TO THE SECOND EDITION

It has been over ten years since I first began writing this book. Back then Ayahuasca was just beginning to become the global medicine that it is today, and the writing of that first manuscript came out of a wish to dispel what I perceived to be some widespread confusion and misunderstanding about this medicine. Ten years later this reason seems to me more valid than ever: the rising popularity of this medicine is an invitation to approach this process with greater responsibility and awareness so that we can keep engaging with it in the future.

In addition to the original manuscript, which was written in order to support people in reaping the most benefits from this medicine while honoring both its traditional Amazonian roots and our present day needs and psychological make-up, I have added two final chapters devoted to our challenges in regards to sustaining a culture of safe and respectful use of this ancestral medicine.

As people in the Amazon need to go further and further into the jungle in order to harvest Ayahuasca vines for the global market, it seems more relevant than ever to approach this medicine aware of the fact that it takes years before this plant can be harvested, as well as the repercussions, ecologic, economic, and cultural, in the Amazon region of our desire to engage with this medicine. One simple way to address the issue of sustainability is not to take this medicine for granted in the same way that we do with any commercial medication or substance, and approach it each and every time with utmost respect and a sincere desire to heal rather than entertain ourselves at the expense of important natural and cultural resources.

In my writing this book there is an implicit trust that we can indeed exercise the necessary maturity and personal responsibility so that this medicine can keep healing and blessing us and our descendants for as long as we may wish, and hopefully this book will help you make sensible choices and consequently make the most of this wonderful medicine.

J.R.

PREFACE

In the mid-1990's I was invited by a friend to attend a ceremony to drink Ayahuasca for the first time. I was quite scared and excited at the same time. I had heard stories from friends who had partaken of this kind of ceremonies before, but my experience of hallucinogens in general and entheogens[2] in particular was rather limited, and the fear of the unknown, of what may or may not happen to me, was quite strong. An aura of mystery and power seemed to surround this medicine.

My guide had recommended I start preparing myself physically for three weeks prior to the ceremony by following a diet without spices and fermented foods, and abstinence from alcohol and recreational drugs. At the same time I started taking a deep look at my own fears and resistances, as well as focusing on my

2 "en-theo-gen" [god within; god- or spirit-facilitating]: a psychoactive sacramental; a plant or chemical substance taken to occasion a connection with the Divine causing a general sensation of coming closer to the Sacred and facilitating self-knowledge and the betterment of the human being.

personal reasons for participating in what was going to be a very profound experience. With a bit of honesty I quickly realized I was not afraid of Ayahuasca itself, but of what it may show me about myself that I may have hidden and repressed in some dark corner of my soul.

On the day of the ceremony we were allowed only breakfast and, by the time I reached the site of our ceremony, my stomach was feeling quite empty. My body was hungry for food while my soul was thirsty for wisdom and healing.

All the participants had gathered in the late afternoon for an introductory talk about the evening ahead and at dusk, after some relaxation exercises, we finally entered the room where the ceremony was to take place. We sat down on mats laid upon the wooden floor like the spokes of a wheel and eventually, one by one, approached our guide to take our cup of this fabled "Vine of the Soul."

I remember distinctly how I felt as I drank my first cup of Ayahuasca: I was like an empty vessel, totally ready to be filled with the healing powers and visions of this medicine – in a place of surrender. Fully aware that there was no turning back, I put aside all worries and opened myself to the best of my abilities to the medicine.

All candles were blown out and we were left in almost complete darkness, with only some low background music to accompany us through our journey. Within twenty minutes I started seeing with my eyes closed the most amazing color patterns I had ever seen, the likeness of which I had only seen before in complex computer-generated images. I was lying down with my head towards the center of our circle and, after what seemed like fifteen minutes of this phantasmagoric light show, I instinctively sat up, reached for the bucket I had prepared next to me for such a situation, and threw up.

It was once I threw up that my journey began in earnest as I started traveling down an endlessly twisting tunnel at an incredible speed, a scary roller coaster ride through all that I had considered until then my "reality." It was not an easy ride: for two hours I was propelled forward while everything around me crumbled to pieces. Anything I would put my attention on, whether it was friends and family, past memories, or the whole planet Earth, would simply explode or vanish. This medicine was causing a relentless but unavoidable disintegration of my ego. It had a disorienting effect and I was scared.

Luckily, a friend had given me a most useful piece of advice for such a situation: whenever fear and panic arises, he had said, just tell yourself and the medicine "I am willing." Over and over again, whenever I realized I was in fear and could find the strength to do so, I would recite this precious mantra; then my ride would come to a short but welcome stop, long enough for me to feel safe, before it would start again.

Every now and then our guide would come by to check on me. To ease my spirit he would sprinkle me with Agua de Florida, a cologne used in South American shamanism. In my altered state of consciousness his face had turned into that of an old and wise Native American medicine man; I could hear his soft voice whisper words of encouragement and I knew I was in good hands.

After two challenging hours of this and with nothing left anywhere around me but some kind of uncomfortable cosmic void, I found myself suddenly sitting on what looked like the top of a northern Californian cliff. I had turned into a giant baby in diapers looking out into the ocean. Shortly thereafter some kind of non-descript board game appeared on the ground in front of me, and a voice told me to look at it and eventually added, "This is your life, and you make the rules."

These few words carried to my consciousness the wisdom I was to receive that night: the knowledge and experience that I was indeed the creator of my own life, not just a pawn in some bizarre cosmic plan but its very source and therefore its master. The implications and consequences of such a revelation were many, but in the heightened state of awareness that I was experiencing, this simple truth shone in all its power and sank deeply into my spirit, not as a simple statement or theory but as a piece of my own truth I would not ever be able to forget.

I spent the rest of the ceremony mimicking the movement of the strange spring-like creatures of all colors that were surrounding me, in a state of unparalleled gratitude, thanking everything and everybody in my life as I had never done before.

It was an amazingly deep experience, and for one whole year I stayed away from all kinds of recreational mind-altering substances. For one thing the experience of drinking Ayahuasca in a ceremonial way had turned off all desires to take mind-altering substances in a recreational, casual way. On the other hand, the experience was so important that it took me that long to integrate it.

It was not until two years later that I drank Ayahuasca again and many more until I first visited Peru for an

Ayahuasca retreat in the Peruvian Amazon jungle: in 2004 I traveled to the Pucallpa area together with a group of other foreigners for an Ayahuasca retreat.

Despite the warnings that this was not going to be a holiday but a challenging experience in the middle of the Amazon, faraway from all the comforts of modern life, I felt right at home and enjoyed my stay there, feeling very much like in a Garden of Eden. The poor diet and consequent pangs of hunger were not easy to embrace, but overall I enjoyed my experience in this amazing environment, totally surrounded by the magical greenery of the jungle and its endless music of insects and animals.

My soul had been aching for quite a while and the retreat proved to be exactly what I needed: the ceremonies were very powerful and the medicine helped me reconnect with myself, letting go of the resentments I had been carrying inside of me for much too long. I left the jungle renewed and once again optimistic about my life and purpose here on this planet.

Two weeks later, as I was approaching the sanctuary of Machu Picchu on the Inca Trail, the rather unexpected thought of studying Amazonian shamanism and plant medicine somehow occurred to me. It left me pretty confused yet excited and curious; so the next year, following a hunch I headed for Iquitos, the largest urban center in the Peruvian Amazon, to work with two different shamans, Don Leoncio Garcia and Don Francisco Montes Shuña. My intention was to see if I really wanted to enter this medicine path or whether it had been just a passing thought.

Traveling this time to the Iquitos area and without anybody I knew, I felt I had gotten myself into more than I had bargained for. I was picked up at the airport by some relatives of Don Leoncio and headed to their small camp a few kilometers from the city. That evening I met with Don Leoncio, an old Shipibo[3] medicine man in his seventies with a smile that instantly dissipated all my concerns and fears. We started drinking Ayahuasca every other day the very next evening. Having had until then only a handful of Ayahuasca experiences under my belt, I quickly forgot my main intention for being there and put all my attention instead towards surviving every ceremony, to the point of even listening to relaxation tapes before each one of them. The first time we drank it was only the two of us and when after a couple of hours he came closer to me to sing I realized I had entered a magical world far away from the familiar rationality of my own Western culture and upbringing – I could either embrace it or resist it. I chose the former without hesitation, and let Don Leoncio's songs envelope me.

It didn't take long for me to make up my mind about my future: during a ceremony I was in such awe of Ayahuasca that I committed myself to working for this amazing medicine that was healing me and opening me up to an experience of life that I had always longed for but somehow had felt was beyond my reach, at least in this lifetime.

Three weeks later I entered Sachamama, the ethnobotanical center created outside Iquitos by Don Francisco Montes Shuña, who was to become my main guide and teacher in the realm of Amazonian plant shamanism. For four weeks under his and

---

3   The Shipibo are an indigenous people living predominantly along the Ucayali River in the Amazon rainforest in Peru.

Kevin Furnas' care I dove deep into the practice of shamanic "diets,"[4] which only confirmed my intention to further study plant medicine, an idea that was quickly becoming a reality for me.

Doors were opening for me effortlessly: during a ceremony there the spirit of the Datura plant (Brugmansia) approached me and offered to teach me all that I needed in order to start doing my work for Ayahuasca. Plants can be quite seductive, and the offer this plant was giving me was enticing and difficult to ignore.

Two months later, after leaving my apartment in Barcelona, Spain, and putting my few belongings into a storage space, I returned to the Pucallpa area for another two-week Ayahuasca retreat. At first I had to face the consequences of my attitude and judgments towards the shaman and the ceremonies there. It didn't take long for the medicine to put me in my place and show me who (or what) was really in charge: during the first ceremony there I experienced an hour-long head-splitting pain in my brain, which had me begging for mercy. I felt like I had been poisoned by the brew, but what I was really experiencing was the effect of my own judgments.

I approached the following four ceremonies with renewed humility and remember distinctly the last one, during which I sat for most of the time on the ground outside the ceremonial space, bathed in moonlight. For the entire duration of the ceremony I was effortlessly surfing on the waves of the medicine's energy, without any resistance or fear. The ten weeks of diet both there and in Iquitos had paid off generously: my body and

---

4   See Chapter 8: Shamanic diets.

spirit had been cleansed of many toxins and I found myself vibrating at a whole new level I had never felt before. Once the heaviness and sorrow I had been carrying with me was dealt with and let go of, I was able to be present, both to others and myself, with renewed enthusiasm and clarity. The physical and emotional purging had affected me deeply and its effects were indeed palpable and ongoing.

I returned to the Cuzco area at the end of October thinking I would return to Iquitos after the following Easter to start working with the Datura plant, but despite my resistances I ended up at Sachamama Ethnobotanical Garden much earlier than I had wished, spending a whole rainy season in the jungle, battling with the ever-present mosquitoes and my recalcitrant ego.

Under Don Francisco and the Datura plant's tutelage I began my apprenticeship, which at this time lasted for five months. With divine help and the support and guidance of my human and plant teachers, I was able to undergo this process, which for me involved primarily a deep cleansing and the taming of my ego. Those were five long months of unsalted foods and endless patience as I hoped the spirit of the Datura plant would fulfill its promise but without seeing any spectacular results until, four months into this shamanic diet, I realized a deep shift inside me had indeed occurred: somehow after much painstaking polishing of the ego, I found myself open to spiritual and celestial energies that up until then had eluded me.

I had unconsciously entered this whole process with images and expectations of being able to learn how to heal people the same way I thought the shamans with whom I had worked did. I knew that they were able to see psychic and subtle physical energies until then obscure to me. I cannot deny that somehow I had fallen prey to the glamour and allure of exotic shamanic practices, but at the same time I was also aware that I had chosen Don Francisco as my teacher precisely because I knew that I didn't have to imitate him but rather develop my own relationship with this medicine as well as my own medicine and healing skills. Eventually I stopped wishing for spectacular shamanic fireworks and began exploring and walking my own path.

Twice a week I would participate in the group ceremonies lead by Don Francisco, and once a week I would drink by myself in order to deepen my connection with the medicine. From the very beginning Ayahuasca told me that on ceremony day I had better skip lunch (and of course dinner) in order to let her work deeper within me, so I left the jungle at the end of the rainy season skinny as can be but radically changed by my experience, confident about my ability to lead people through the often choppy waters of Ayahuasca ceremonies, and with all the basic tools and the awareness necessary to support people in their healing process.

My commitment to making this medicine available in the best possible way to all the people who feel drawn to its healing powers is also what has eventually guided and driven me to write this book. I hope you find it a valuable guide for the journey ahead.

INTRODUCTION

This book is primarily directed to those people who are interested in drinking Ayahuasca but have little or no familiarity with it, as well as for those people who, despite various experiences with this medicine, haven't quite found the answers or have failed to achieve the results they were looking for.

In the years since I have been leading healing Ayahuasca ceremonies, I have noticed the incredible importance of adequately informing and supporting people throughout their process. As part of this process I share my view as to how I personally feel this medicine best benefits us and recommend the best way to approach it.

In my own work as an ayahuasquero, a lot of the preparatory work with my clients, apart from recommending certain dietary restrictions, revolves around the focusing and formulating of one's intentions for each ceremony and then offering the support in dealing with whatever resistances may arise during the process. Last but not least, we have some time the morning after each ceremony for sharing and processing the experience in order to clarify possible confusions and facilitate the integration process.

All of these aspects seem to me of the utmost importance for people drinking Ayahuasca, but who are not native of the Amazon basin and therefore unfamiliar with its ways and symbols. The cultural gap and the resulting misconceptions, when not addressed and reframed, are often key factors between an experience that is confusing and dissatisfying, and a positive and healing one.

In my work with foreigners I have found the best approach to be one that fully honors the native traditional use of Ayahuasca and also acknowledges the cultural and psychological makeup and needs of those who drink it. Nowadays more and more people from all walks of life and spiritual and religious backgrounds feel drawn to this medicine in often surprising ways. The use of Ayahuasca has left the boundaries of the Amazon basin where it comes from, and has become in the last thirty years a medicine known and used worldwide.

The power of this brew aroused the curiosity of the first ethnobotanists who explored the Amazon region, such as Richard Evans Schultes. Then in 1953 the American novelist William Burroughs traveled to South America in search of Ayahuasca, resulting in the publication in 1963 of The Yagé Letters, co-authored with Allen Ginsberg.

In 1971, Terrence McKenna and his brother Dennis traveled to the Colombian Amazon looking for DMT-containing preparations. This subsequent journey and his experiences in South America turned Terrence into the most vocal supporter for Ayahuasca and DMT, an alkaloid present in the Ayahuasca brew, popularizing their virtues both in print and speech. It was thus that Ayahuasca entered the Western psyche.

Following the decline of the revolutionary and terrorist organization Sendero Luminoso (Shining Path) in the early 1990's, Peru has quickly become a very popular tourist destination, in particular for those interested in mysticism and spirituality. The designation of Machu Picchu as one of the new Seven Wonders of the World has furthered the image of Peru as a must-see country.

The development of the tourist industry has certainly facilitated the access to previously hard-to-reach destinations, and this has been a mostly positive phenomenon for both visitors and native populations. However, the drinking of Ayahuasca has turned into a kind of industry, to the point that it is quite easy to find someone almost anywhere in the Amazon jungle willing to give a visitor some Ayahuasca to drink. This sometimes occurs without any questions or preparations, much to the detriment of the person drinking it. Over the years I have heard many tales of people drinking Ayahuasca that was at best mediocre in quality and strength, or with people who would go to sleep soon after administering the brew, often leaving the unfortunate participants to their own devices in totally unknown territories, both physical and psychic.

Ayahuasca is a very powerful medicine that ought to be taken with respect and under the right conditions, otherwise its indiscriminate use can turn into a dangerous and often confusing experience, rather than an enlightening one. It is with this in mind that I have decided to write this book, so that people interested in drinking Ayahuasca can profit the most from this experience and return to it whenever they feel the need or desire.

Shamanism is not about blindly following dogmas, but more about learning through one's own direct experience and following one's intuition. There is a vast range of traditions, each belonging to a different ethnic group, geographical area, and historical moment, as well as vast bodies of knowledge associated with the medicinal and spiritual use of Ayahuasca. And yet, all this knowledge is of questionable value until its validity is proven through personal experience.

My own training under Don Francisco Montes, an indigenous medicine man of Capanahua descent, and a few other medicine people in the Peruvian Amazon has no pretense of being purist nor totally exhaustive. Don Francisco is actually particularly fond of reminding everyone who works with him that this is a science that has no end. It was never my intention to "go native," but always clear that my role in working with this medicine was that of a bridge between the traditional, cultural, and spiritual worlds of Amazonian plant shamanism and the Western/modern psyche. The insights of this book have been shaped not only by what I have learned in the jungle and by supporting hundreds of people from around the world through their healing and spiritual processes, but also by my own cultural and spiritual background and interests. Hopefully the viewpoints expressed here will help the reader deepen their connection with this medicine.

One can easily end up spending more time in or around Iquitos and elsewhere talking about this or that way of using Ayahuasca rather than actually drinking it. Everybody, from shamans to laypeople, seems to have a clear opinion regarding the best way, the only way, or the traditional way of working with this medicine in particular and plant medicine in general. It strikes me as ironic that despite how deeply we claim Ayahuasca has affected us, that we don't seem capable of restraining ourselves from one of the most insidious obstacles to spiritual evolution, i.e., passing judgment.

Most likely there never was one single, unique, divinely inspired way of working with Ayahuasca. If there was ever such a thing, then it quickly morphed into many different versions and, considering the lack of historical records and evidence in the jungle, we can leave our minds in peace because we will never be able to validate with absolute certainty any single claim or theory: people are simply doing their best to keep a tradition alive that, like so many aspects of life in the Amazon, is at risk of disappearing.

This book makes no claim of wanting to be the definite and last word on Ayahuasca. It is a book clearly intended for non-natives and written by someone born and raised far from the Amazon basin. All suggestions and recommendations come from my own personal experience in working with this medicine. Feel free to simply dismiss any part of it if it fails to resonate with you.

In the end shamanism is an empirical discipline where the validity of any assumption needs to be tested by each individual. What works for many isn't necessarily true for all and at times we are called to travel the road less traveled and even break a few ancient taboos in order to keep the tradition alive and dynamic. I agree that traditional ways offer us a wealth of information and wisdom, but also feel that in order to flourish any tradition should maintain a certain degree of flexibility and welcome the occasional questioning of the validity of its ways so that it may continue to properly nourish the spirit of the tribe. My only advice in this regard is to always be willing to take full responsibility for the consequences of our actions, whether we decide to follow someone else's advice or the voice of our own heart.

Unlike humans, plants have little interest in dogma, and so we are witnessing the transformation of Ayahuasca as a sacrament for various kinds of rituals and ceremonies among greatly diverse cultures and spiritual traditions. We can only speculate as to the reasons for this phenomenon, one of them possibly being that Ayahuasca seems to be an ideal medicine, both deep and vast in its effects, to help us deal with the problems affecting humanity and the planet at this moment in history. Considering the huge task at hand of healing thousands of years of abuse and the resulting wounds to both the human race and the Earth as a whole, it seems that Ayahuasca has made its entrance in the global psyche not a moment too soon.

DISCLAIMER

This book is intended for informational purposes only. People wishing to drink Ayahuasca should consult their medical doctors before engaging with this medicine.

The use, possession, and trafficking of Ayahuasca is illegal in many countries, and the author doesn't condone the breaking of the laws of any country.

WHAT IS AYAHUASCA?

The term "Ayahuasca" is a Quechua name that re-
fers to the plant *Banisteriopsis Caapi*, a vine native
to the Amazon rainforest, as well as to any of the various infusions or decoctions prepared from the same
plant and used for shamanic, medicinal, religious, and
spiritual purposes.

The vine contains the beta-carboline harmala
alkaloids and monoamine oxidase inhibitors (MAOIs)
harmine, harmaline, and tetrahydroharmine. Although
recipes vary from area to area, the brew known as
Ayahuasca (or "Yagé" in Colombia) is usually made
from this vine and another plant containing DMT
(N,N-dimethyltryptamine), a powerful hallucinogenic
alkaloid which is active orally only when combined
with an MAOI. The most common DMT-rich plants used
in the Peruvian Amazon jungle are *Psychotria viridis*
("Chakruna" in Quechua) and *Diplopterys cabrerana*
(also known as "Chagropanga," "Chaliponga," or
"Huambisa").

Even though according to the Western viewpoint DMT is the active principle in the brew, Amazonian shamans believe that it is the Ayahuasca vine that is the real healer, "la planta maestra": traditionally, the ingestion of Ayahuasca is not about having the extraordinary visions that have made this medicine popular and mythical, but primarily about cleansing, healing, and connecting with our own truths, wisdom, and intelligence.

My own personal feeling is that the Ayahuasca vine works primarily on the peripheral and enteric nervous system, a clear sign of this being the intense diarrhea it often produces, whereas the DMT-containing ingredients affect the central nervous system as indicated by the strong effects on the visual cortex, and the feeling of the medicine reaching every part of one's physical body and the not-uncommon experience of being "rewired."

The brew is prepared by cutting and smashing portions of the vine, and soaking them overnight in water together with the Chakruna plant. They are then boiled for several hours until a thick, syrupy liquid is obtained. Each shaman will add his or her own touch to the brew, often including other ingredients to the basic recipe, such as Datura (*Brugmansia*) or jungle Tobacco (*Nicotiana rustica*).

Ayahuasca is commonly known in the Amazon basin as "la purga," the purge. The strong vomit-inducing properties of this medicine make it a well-deserved title. But the purgative effects of Ayahuasca do not end here. Under the ego-dissolving effects of this medicine we become once again aware that the separation between body, mind, and spirit is only in our heads, i.e., a trick of the mind; so the cleansing action of Ayahuasca is one that encompasses the entirety of our being: in our physical body, in the emotional body, the mind, the soul, and the spirit. This is a reality experienced by almost every person who has taken this medicine.

Due to its cleansing properties, drinking Ayahuasca involves first and foremost the openness of one's heart and mind to letting go of all those things that we carry within that may have been important or even necessary to our physical and emotional survival, but no longer serve us in the present time and have actually become obstacles to our very own development and evolution.

We spend our lives gathering objects, experiences, and relationships. We also learn ways to cope with certain situations: sometimes the emotions sparked by certain experiences are too intense or painful, or the environment in which we find ourselves is not supportive of the full expression of certain emotional states, for instance in the case of the loss of someone dear. So we learn to repress certain emotions, sometimes to the point of denying them. Traumatic or challenging experiences that have not been given full permission to be experienced are left half-baked in our psyche: we carry their weight without knowing that healing and letting go are available to us if we are only shown how. Living life while carrying so much emotional and mental baggage can be difficult if not impossible: we go to this medicine asking for healing and this is what it delivers.

When I think of Ayahuasca, the most immediate image that comes to mind is that of snakes of light. The snake is a universal symbol of healing and medicine, and in the Andean cosmology it is also the king of the

Underworld, which to me is everything right underneath the Earth's crust and therefore represents the immense healing and nurturing energies of the Earth itself.

As a cosmic symbol of the divine Kundalini,[5] this snake speaks of the infinite potential and energies that lie dormant at the very root of our being. Similar to the uncoiled Kundalini that reaches from the bottom of our spine in classical Tantric descriptions, the Ayahuasca vine grows from the ground towards the top of the jungle canopy where its main nutrient, sunshine, lies aplenty.

Plants have the unique characteristic of being able to synthesize from light most of the energy they need for living and thriving – they are practically made of light. Translating this image on a personal level, I feel that the Ayahuasca vine is a mirror of the human condition, born in the depth of the womb and forever reaching for the Divine Light represented by the sun. For me the drinking of Ayahuasca is always the ingestion of Pure Light that brings light, lightness, and enlightenment to the darkest and heaviest parts of my being so I can live my life more fully and in accordance with my divine nature.

---

5   Kundalini is described in various Indian spiritual traditions as an indwelling spiritual energy that can be awakened in order to purify the subtle system and ultimately to bestow the state of Yoga, or Divine Union. Its awakening is oftentimes experienced as a release of physical and psychic energy.

TWO AYAHUASCA LEGENDS

O nce upon a time there lived in the jungle a beautiful young maiden. Every day at sunset she would
go to a clearing by the river to bathe and nothing
pleased her more than to wash using the leaves of a
Chakruna bush that grew nearby.

Every day she would scrub her body with the
Chakruna leaves, singing and praising their qualities
and soft feel on her skin. Her devotion to that plant
grew so much that one day the Chakruna bush started
speaking to her, thus saying, "Dear lady, you have been
so nice and grateful to me that I want to reciprocate
your gratitude by revealing a secret to you no other
human has ever known, and one that your people will
treasure forever. You see that snake-like vine wrapping
itself around that tree over there? Well, if you mix my
leaves with that vine and cook them for hours, you will
prepare a drink that will open your spirit to the secrets

of this jungle and heal your body of all your aches and ills."

And so it was that the magical mixture of Ayahuasca was revealed to our ancestors in the jungle.

It is told in the jungle that a long time ago a very powerful medicine man, not content with his knowledge, which was already very vast, called his entire clan to his house. There, in front of everybody, he vowed to sit in meditation until the deepest secrets of the jungle would be revealed to him. That very night he went and sat against a tree. He sat there, motionlessly, in deep meditation. The food his family would bring to him, he would not touch and the dogs would eat. The water his beloved wife would leave by his side he would not touch. Days and weeks went by, the shaman was slowly withering until one day his breath was no longer with him and life seemed to have left his body.

Following his instructions, his body was left where he had been sitting until one day, to the surprise of all the villagers, out of his limbs now decaying started sprouting the first shoots of what was to become the very first Ayahuasca vine on Earth.

The Amazon jungle is a land of legends and myths. The lack of a written tradition is more than compensated for by an abundantly rich oral tradition, where wisdom, knowledge, and traditions are passed down from generation to generation.

To enter the Amazon jungle is to visit another world, a different dimension where events take on different meanings than in westernized cultures. It was during my first Ayahuasca ceremony with a Shipibo shaman outside Iquitos that I realized I had to leave my westerly ways behind and embrace without judgment or preconceived ideas what was happening to me: I was entering a magic world where most of my education and thought patterns were pretty useless.

One of the questions that has haunted many, me included, is how did humans discover the recipe for the Ayahuasca brew? The Ayahuasca vine and the Chakruna plant bear no resemblance and don't grow together. Considering the incredible variety of Amazonian flora, it would take millennia of scientific trial and error before discovering such a powerful combination.

The two myths here succinctly told give us an idea of the relationship between humans and their environment in the Amazon jungle. In the first one we become aware of a fact that is one of the principal tenets of Amazonian shamanism: plants are living entities and capable of communication, and often in connection with humans.

Chinese medicine and folk medicine around the world make use of the distinctive traits of each plant as a way of interpreting and deciphering their properties. Intuition is often the key in understanding the ways of Nature. In Amazonian shamanism, in particular through the "dieta" process, the concept is taken even further: by engaging in a special diet and drinking extracts of a particular plant, humans enter in direct connection and communication with plants, their energy, and spirit. This may be a way of not only reconnecting with plants and Nature, but also with our ancestral capacity to do so and walk upon this Earth as integral parts of it and no longer alienated from it.

The other important aspect of the first story is the fact that the main human character is a woman. Despite the fact that nowadays the majority of shamans are male, this tale reminds us that women are naturally connected with the powers of Nature. In patriarchal cultures this original role of healers and shamans has been taken away from women, and in today's race for equality most women still struggle to reconnect with the energies of Nature that run so deeply in their very being, but from which they have been long alienated in the course of human history.

In this first myth our Amazonian Eve is shown the Tree of Knowledge. This does not result in her expulsion from the Garden of Eden, but on the contrary, it leads to a deeper connection with its energies: since the beginning of its use, Ayahuasca has become the key in Amazonian shamanism and culture to access both the secrets of the Forest and the mysteries of the Spirit.

In the second myth another very interesting aspect of the connection between humans and Nature is described. Here it is Man himself to become the first Ayahuasca vine, stressing the interconnectedness between all things and creatures on the planet. In the wider vision of Amazonian spirituality there is no hierarchy between species: all creatures have their own place in the vast design of Creation. It is a fluid universe where the unity of all living beings means not only their reciprocal interconnection but also facilitates their communication and identity. In the same way that a shaman can take on the appearance and moves of a jaguar or an eagle, he can also turn into a vine. And so the vine embodies the highest of human qualities: wisdom.

The myth also illustrates the deep connection of humans and the vine of Ayahuasca, to the point of a total identity between the two. It indicates to which extent the use of Ayahuasca is important to the people of the jungle: Ayahuasca, as the transformation of a shaman, who is one of the most important figures in jungle societies, is also able to reflect back to humans their highest potential and spiritual nature. Drinking Ayahuasca then becomes not only a way of connecting with a plant spirit, but also with the knowledge and wisdom of all of humanity as well as the medicine people that have worked with it throughout history.

PAST AND PRESENT USE:

THE ROLE OF AYAHUASCA IN THE AMAZON BASIN YESTERDAY AND TODAY; AYAHUASCA IN THE WORLD TODAY

According to oral tradition and the few written materials available to us today,[6] shamans and Amazon natives have been using Ayahuasca for thousands of years. Ayahuasca is the central spiritual sacrament for many ethnic groups in the Amazon basin, the main technique of ecstasy and spiritual trance for shamans all over the jungle.

It is referred to as the "Mother of all Plants" in that it provides shamans with a way of communicating and interacting with all the other plant teachers and medicines of the jungle, as well as other energies and spirits of the Earth and the Heavens.

In tribal ceremonies Ayahuasca is said to have also been used to create a telepathic connection among its members, as well as the energies and spirits of the jungle – because of this, the first ethnobotanists called the active ingredient in Ayahuasca "telepathine." During Ayahuasca ceremonies, the participants would connect with animal spirits to find better hunting grounds, and with plant spirits for healing, as well as the source of imbalances that may be affecting the tribe.

Another important aspect of Ayahuasca use is the reconnection not only with the spirit world, populated with power animals, spirits of Nature, heavenly energies, and extraterrestrial beings, but also with the spirits of ancestors and the spirit of the tribe. As an ego-dissolving substance, Ayahuasca enhances the unity of the tribe members and facilitates their cohesion and sense of community.

---

6 See Bruce F. Lamb's books: *Wizard of the Upper Amazon: the story of Manuel Cordova-Rios*, and *Rio Tigre and beyond: the Amazon Jungle Medicine of Manuel Cordova-Rios*, both published by North Atlantic Books.

Today mestizo communities, which account for the majority of the Amazon population, use Ayahuasca mostly for healing purposes, both physical and spiritual. Sometimes it is only the shaman that drinks Ayahuasca in order to find and cure the ills afflicting the patient. In other occasions both shaman and patient drink the brew.

The use of Ayahuasca is definitely a science, but also an art that varies greatly from region to region and even among medicine people of the same area. The people who insist on claiming to know and own the only way of using this medicine ought to be looked upon with some suspicion: as in all spiritual traditions, the paths may differ greatly but the ultimate destination remains the same.

In the last couple of centuries and with the migration of outsiders into jungle territories, Amazonian shamanism has moved beyond the boundaries of remote tribes. On the one hand there has been a renaissance in the connection between medicine people from the jungle and those from the Andean region, a connection that has always been strong since the dawn of civilization with a constant exchange of goods and knowledge, but more recently radically facilitated by improved traveling conditions. On the other hand a new breed of shamans, called "vegetalistas," has come into existence. These are people not necessarily native from the jungle but trained in the ways of Amazonian shamanism and plant medicine. Vegetalistas are often seen working in more urban areas, both within and out the Amazon basin. By working within a different social context, their work primarily involves healing.

Another interesting phenomenon of Ayahuasca use is the birth of new Christian-based churches that use Ayahuasca as their main sacrament. Best known among them are the Church of Santo Daime and the União do Vegetal, both originally from Brazil and created by Brazilian rubber tappers working in the Amazon region. These churches have developed rituals quite different from the ones in the shamanic tradition but seem to provide their members with a very valuable experience nonetheless.

As a matter of fact a myriad of ways of using Ayahuasca has seen the light of day recently: in the wake of post-modernity and neo-shamanism we can now participate in ceremonies and retreats that combine the use of Ayahuasca with elements of Christian or Buddhist teachings, psychotherapy, and countless other disciplines.

This may also be interpreted as part of a global phenomenon that calls for the respectful sharing of native knowledge, once kept secret but now being exchanged for the benefit of all humanity. To the purist's eye, the mixing of different cultural traditions may seem like blasphemy, but to the visionary it is proof of a simple yet important fact: the spirit of Ayahuasca is now engaged in working with as many people as possible, quickly moving out of its native territory to become a globally available medicine that speaks different languages in order to be better understood by larger groups of people.

After my last visit to the jungle to study with my teacher and listening to him, I can see how important it is to remain aware that no matter how far this medicine has travelled beyond the Amazon jungle, Ayahuasca is not just a brew or a chemical compound, but an energy that carries within it a whole world, physical, psychic, and spiritual. To hold this awareness with utmost respect seems to me particularly important the more widespread and popular this medicine becomes.

HEALING AND AYAHUASCA FOR THE 21ST CENTURY

The concepts of healing, and emotional and spiritual health have evolved over the course of millennia, particularly in the West and in all cultures touched for better or worse by its influence. Since the birth of hypnosis and psychoanalysis, our perception of what it is to be human has been shifting progressively towards models and interpretations that are more and more holistic rather than the mechanistic view imposed by the scientific method that began in the 1700's. Instead of a machine that simply needed to be well oiled in order to perform optimally, the idea of the human physiological and psychological experience has broadened and deepened. This began with the introduction of the concept of the unconscious, both individual and collective. When one considers the influence of viable notions such as reincarnation, karmic realities, and extrasensory perception, which all led to the human potential movement, as well as transpersonal and depth psychology, we see a vastly expanded model of being. This evolution and philosophical expansion would not have happened without the respectful exposure that Western culture has had with Native cultures and philosophies from around the world.

The mainstream ideologies of the Judeo-Christian tradition of the West had been for a long time centered around an increasing demonization of the physical body and its natural drives, of sexuality, and of the Feminine in general – and one could easily affirm that one of the main benefits of the scientific revolution has at least been the freedom to challenge and discuss openly such ancient beliefs and dogmas without getting burned at the stake. During the many centuries of Christian religious supremacy in Europe, the mind had become mainly an instrument of severe self-repression and guilt-inducing thought patterns, constantly working to drive deeper and deeper into the unconscious those aspects of human life considered immoral and sinful by the religious authorities. Excessive repression leads eventually to rebellion, and in the last two centuries we have benefitted from the birth of many liberation movements that have reclaimed the natural dignity of women, gay people, racial minorities, as well as native populations all over the world. As a whole the shift has been towards greater and greater acceptance and recognition of humanity in all its expressions. As a result the concept of healing has moved from the need to "fix" and conform to one of acceptance and celebration of the many expressions of the human experience. In this light, health and healing have become synonyms of wholeness and the intrinsic holiness of every individual and social or ethnic group.

The use of Ayahuasca has therefore become one of the many tools to recover and remember such wholeness and holiness: by letting go of old wounds and judgments we are once again able to accept, love, and celebrate who we are in our totality. The contemporary use of Ayahuasca applied to such goals is deeply indebted not only to the survival of valuable traditional healing methods, but also to the development in the 1950's and 1960's of therapeutic work which combined established modes of psychotherapy with mind-altering substances (such as Mescaline and LSD) and altered states of consciousness in general.[7] These therapeutic modalities, which were developed to assist individuals in recovering and healing deeply concealed traumas and even past-life occurrences, became the groundbreaking guidelines for many subsequent healing therapies such as Gestalt, Rebirthing, Holotropic Breathwork, and many forms of neo-shamanism.

These new healing modalities are not only meant for healing but also support our reconnection to the transpersonal and the transcendental. The importance of reconnecting with our own divinity and the sacredness of Life as part of our path toward health and wholeness is being recognized more and more, and so the mystical visions and deeply spiritual experiences and awakenings that one can achieve by engaging with Ayahuasca are totally in alignment with our most recent discoveries of what it means to be healthy today.

---

7   For those interested in this subject, the work and books by Stanislav Grof are particularly recommended.

HOW AYAHUASCA WORKS:

CHEMISTRY AND SOUL THERAPY

Despite the claims and advances of modern medicine and science, we are actually quite ignorant about the mechanisms of the brain in particular, and the connection between the physical body and the spirit in general. Somehow the psyche, consciousness, and the Life force are aspects of our Universe that continue to elude even the finest of our scientists. Or maybe they are simply beyond the realm of traditional science as we have known it for the last few centuries. Models meant to provide an understanding of our own reality and existence, continue to evolve: they are the final answer to our queries, yet far from being written.

In terms of chemistry, the two main ingredients of the Ayahuasca brew act synergistically: the dimethyltryptamines alkaloids in the Chakruna plant are prevented from breaking down in the digestive tract by the harmine and and harmaline present in the Ayahuasca vine. Dimethyltryptamine (DMT) is a naturally occurring compound of the tryptamine family, very similar to monoamine neurotransmitters like serotonin and other psychedelic compounds such as psilocin, the active molecule of psilocybin.

Because of the close resemblance to serotonin, there is a risk of overloading the system with neurotransmitters with possible negative results. Therefore people who are under medical treatment of all sorts of antidepressants and medications that affect the nervous system are highly discouraged from drinking Ayahuasca until at least three months after discontinuing the use of these medications. This is particularly important in the case of SSRIs (Selective Serotonin Reuptake Inhibitors), a class of antidepressants used in the treatment of depression and anxiety disorders. Among these medications are Prozac, Fluctin, Celexa, and Zoloft. By the way, I have witnessed how the use of Ayahuasca to treat chronic depression, where the illness is so deep reaching that brain chemistry is affected, is often a very lengthy process and not one where success is always guaranteed.

Otherwise there are no restrictions to drinking Ayahuasca: this is a natural medicine, and easily metabolized by the body, DMT being a naturally occurring substance, produced in small quantities by the pineal gland in the brain as well. Its ingestion causes no hangovers, chemical or psychological addiction, or post-use "downs," unlike most recreational drugs popular today. The "Hoasca Project" study conducted in Brazil in the early 1990's has actually reported as part of its findings that the use of Ayahuasca improves the body's ability to produce serotonin, quite unlike drugs like cocaine and ecstasy, which in the long run not only deplete this important neurotransmitter but also weakens the ability of the body to produce it.

What is more interesting are the ways this medicine acts on the human spirit and consciousness: without strict scientific methods, we can examine how Ayahuasca works on the spirit mostly on an empirical basis by looking at its effects on those who drink it.

Shadow And Light

Ayahuasca, like other entheogens such as Peyote, San Pedro cactus (Huachuma) or LSD, acts as a powerful mirror, capable of reflecting back to us our most hidden and best-kept secrets: not only the ones we are ashamed of, but also the beautiful ones we are somehow uncomfortable with – our talents, gifts, and real passions.[8] To the drinker of Ayahuasca these revelations fall into two different categories, which for the sake of convenience I will refer to as "the shadow," and "the light."

If there is one truly powerful quality of Ayahuasca, it is its ability to confront us with those aspects of our personalities we'd rather not see at all: past unhealed traumas, repressed memories, denied dynamics and emotions, and so on. We have become experts at repressing what C.G. Jung called "the shadow," using every possible stratagem in order to disown those parts of ourselves we are not particularly proud of or comfortable with. These survival tricks are often necessary in order to cope with difficult events and situations, but they are useful only in the short run: repressing painful events and emotions only drive them deeper into our being, and their unconscious presence only make them more powerful, pervasive, and noxious. Manifestations of such defense mechanisms range from denial and dissociation to the presence of entities that are perceived as foreign intrusions into one's psyche but are actually put into place by the individual in order to protect oneself from even coming close to re-experiencing situations and emotions similar to old unresolved traumas. Holding on to certain patterns and beliefs actually colors how we feel about ourselves, others, and everything we do, whether we are aware of it or not.

For instance, in the case of the loss of a loved one, it is not at all uncommon, particularly in our

---

8   The process is similar to looking at a landscape through a window at the end of the day: as darkness falls upon the world outside, our own image reflected in the window becomes more and more prominent until it is all that is visible.

modern society, that the grieving process is denied, maybe because the environment is not supportive or because we feel that we need to be strong in order to support others in these difficult times. So, the grieving process, which in traditional societies is an integral part of their cultures and lifestyles, is never really allowed to happen. The grief, sadness, and anger that often accompany the death of someone dear to us are then suppressed rather than expressed and released. As a consequence of this suppression we find ourselves carrying these emotions deep within ourselves, and often end up dreading the sudden departure of other people from our lives because of the additional pain of not being able to grieve them properly. The work with Ayahuasca often provides the space for the expression of such emotions and the resulting cathartic release.

Mankind is called today to bring light and awareness onto all aspects of existence, particularly those regarding our inner lives, bringing healing and integration to old wounds and unresolved issues. By bringing back to our conscious awareness deeply resisted experiences, Ayahuasca allows us to begin in earnest a healing process that is long overdue, both individually and collectively.

During an Ayahuasca ceremony we often come face to face with our shadow, and frequently we encounter issues we are all too familiar with: those things that will simply not go away, no matter how much therapy of any kind we have undergone. It is exactly the desire to heal these stubborn and painful aspects of our consciousness that brings us to the Ayahuasca experience. And the medicine, when the individual is ready for what it has to offer, rarely disappoints: it brings us straight to the point of the matter, showing us the wounds we have come to heal, and supporting us in the healing process. The expanded state of consciousness brought on by the ingestion of Ayahuasca not only brings our issues to the surface, but also allows us to perceive them from new and profoundly unique perspectives, thus facilitating their acceptance, understanding, and integration. This is not a purely mental process but one that implies our full presence and attention in order to not merely think about them, but also to explicitly and directly feel these resisted experiences: because of the temporary abatement of the ego and its judging mechanisms, we are finally free to experience events and emotions that the ego had previously deemed as too painful or overwhelming.

The use of the mind is the easiest way to distance oneself from experience; rational thinking can be helpful in understanding certain aspects of our behavior, but actually becomes a hindrance when healing is sought. The expanded state of consciousness of Ayahuasca genuinely takes us out of our ordinary rational mind-state and into the feeling-state necessary for the healing and integration process. In our normal conscious mind we tend to interpret events and relationships always in the same way – it is a prerogative of the mind to always want to be right and fairly rigid in its viewpoint.

Recently a friend of mine who had suffered for many years from feeling rejected and estranged from his father had a most amazing experience during a ceremony: his dead father appeared to him and explained to him how he had actually never rejected him, telling him how, had he truly rejected him, he would have thrown him out of his house and disowned him altogether. He went on to tell him that the reason for his attitude towards his own son had been simply because he didn't understand him and didn't know how to deal with him. These revelations allowed my friend to reframe his whole relationship with his father under a new light, and made the way for a whole new level of understanding, compassion, and forgiveness towards him. The relaxing of the mind's activity allows for a letting go of previously held judgments and viewpoints so that an expanded viewpoint can arise.

ALTERED STATES OF CONSCIOUSNESS

Letting go of our usual ways is not always an easy route: we are so used to living almost exclusively within the rational dimension that altered states of consciousness often bring up all sorts of issues regarding one's ability to navigate through life, if only for a few hours, without a fully functioning mind that operates in a familiar way. Western people particularly have difficulty surrendering the rational mind, and expanded states of consciousness are often experienced as threatening to the individual as well as society. Our identification with the mind and the ego is so deep that their temporary banishment from our field of awareness is often perceived as a kind of death and brings about all sorts of fears regarding one's own survival and well-being. When it comes to modern man, this is perhaps what the word "Ayahuasca" primarily means: the "Vine of Death." This implies for many individuals the (mostly temporary) death of the ego, i.e., the dissolution of what one has come to think of as oneself.

More often than not the death one experiences is the final letting go and release of aspects of our own personalities that we have been carrying despite the fact that they are no longer truly useful or valid. Because the ego hangs on to those dynamics for its own survival, their demise is perceived as a little death. Our uneasiness with the dying and letting go processes, whether physical or psychological, can turn this phenomenon into a difficult experience: no matter how much we say we want to let go of certain things, the actuality of the process can be met with all sorts of both conscious and unconscious resistances. Luckily, Ayahuasca gently yet powerfully supports us in the letting go process unlike any other medicine – that is its magic. To be able to let go of old beliefs and viewpoints enables us to be truly in the present moment instead of experiencing what is in front of us through the often distorting lens of the past, or through the thick layers of our fears and worries. The present moment, when fully lived and openly embraced, is the realm of absolute transformation, of endless possibilities, which extend far beyond our imagination.

I will never forget the first time I had such an experience thanks to Ayahuasca. The ceremony had already been closed but I was still in the throes of the medicine and someone's remark drove me straight into one of my most uncomfortable scenarios: the feeling of not being seen for who I am. I was experiencing a lot of anger and frustration, but unable to move or do anything. I wanted to leave the ceremonial space and go scream out my anger away from everybody else, but couldn't. Finally I had this moment of clarity and honesty, and could see how this whole scenario was all of my own doing, and that I was not only the main actor but also the screenwriter, director, and location manager. I leaned back and marveled at the intricacy of this whole movie I had created for myself over and over until I violently threw up. I was still shaking from the experience when Don José approached me. He sprinkled me with Camalonga (*Thevetia Peruviana*) water, but with my eyes closed it felt like I was being showered with a bright light. Taking full responsibility for my own drama caused the paradigm I had created and fed throughout the years to finally crack and fall apart. The sense of liberation and elation that followed this piercing and puncturing through of one of my most limiting creations was extraordinary: it was as if heavy chains, which had turned out to be of my own design and manufacture, had finally broken off my soul. I never fell asleep that night, but instead spent my time imagining and contemplating all the wonderful things I could do now that I was no longer trapped in this old scenario that had kept me feeling small and unappreciated all my life.

The last time such an important shift happened was during my most recent shamanic diet. This time the theme was a similar one: feeling judged as not good enough. In my mind I knew I was making all this up and quickly realized that if I wanted to move forward in my spiritual path, I had to gather all my strength and courage and let this old story go. When the final letting go of a story happens, it can be rather quick and sudden. Yet, the relative simplicity of the process often belies months, years, or lifetimes of preparatory work as we deal with stubborn resistances and attachments to past events and identities. So I drank Ayahuasca and did all that I could do to let go of this belief of being judged rather than accepted and loved. It was only the next day that the result of this letting go shone in all its glory: the space that had been previously occupied by the belief and subsequent experience of being looked at by critical eyes was now filled with a lightness and openness where a much deeper personal truth and reality could shine. This deeper truth was that the Divine loves me and everybody else equally and unconditionally, and that this has always been and will always be so. To allow myself to be enveloped by Divine Love, despite the years of longing for it, was something that could not have happened had I chosen to hold on to the conflicting belief of being judged and not loved enough.

It is really just our own attachment to old limited views of our existence that keeps us locked in nightmares of pain and separation. When we are finally ready to let go of our own preconceived limited views of ourselves and the world, then we can begin to taste the endless energy that springs from Divine Source and drink from it freely.

The state of egolessness, the drastic change in self-image, and the inability of the mind to control the experience can be a truly challenging experience for some. When overwhelming and without the proper environment and support, the experience can become even traumatic. This is not due to some kind of inherent danger of Ayahuasca, but perhaps to the poor preparation of the individual who has ingested it, and the inability to surrender to the medicine.

There is a lot of discussion these days about the power of surrender, and it has been my own experience that there are several layers of surrender and resistance before a total letting go is possible. The demise of the ego puts us in touch with the All, and it is easy for us to feel overwhelmed and scared by such power and immensity. A few years ago I was drinking medicine by myself and was asking the Earth to help me with a particularly bad health situation. And yet, despite my request I realized in the process that there was a part of me still afraid of letting myself be totally embraced and nurtured by Mother Earth. The fear of loss of one's individuality is often much greater than one can possibly assume.

The use of plant medicines and other entheogens can offer serious reality checks on how truly willing we are to surrender. That can be a humbling but always insightful and important experience. Modern Western society has so thoroughly condemned these states of consciousness that we have become totally alienated from them, to the point that when we are exposed to them we easily feel at a loss, often reacting with panic or unreasonable behaviors. To most traditional societies and according to our most sacred texts, the rational brain is only one part of the human experience – the realms of the spirit and its mysteries are actually what many cultures consider as our true nature. Yet, the use of entheogens, one of the most direct ways of accessing such dimensions, has not only been demonized by various establishments, but also relegated to some kind of intellectual limbo where all sensible discussion is avoided and frowned upon. Perhaps this is due to the fact that these experiences are often beyond the realm of words and left-brain reasoning patterns – the great abyss beyond which we have confined non-ordinary states of consciousness is often a difficult one to bridge.

For the person drinking Ayahuasca for the first time, familiarity with these other states of consciousness, either through the use of other entheogens, meditation, or other spiritual practices, is often a welcome bonus but not a requisite. What is necessary in my opinion is a willingness to let go of preconceived ideas about oneself and the world because often Ayahuasca reflects back to us an image of the Universe that is radically different from the one we are used to. It is not that we have to change our belief systems, but just be flexible enough to make space for these other visions and viewpoints without panicking. People with a rigid personality and very attached to their beliefs will find Ayahuasca rather unbearable and are discouraged from using it. And preconceived negative attitudes towards "drugs" or "primitive cultures" aren't helpful either. The use of Ayahuasca isn't for everyone: it is a challenging medicine that requires an open mind and a willingness to surrender to its mysterious ways. This cannot be stressed often enough.

In Western culture, surrender is perceived as defeat and weakness – the ego, so constantly intent on controlling every situation and environment, is reluctant to let go and get out of the picture. "Control" - physical, emotional, and spiritual - has become our way of life. Ayahuasca forces the individual to let go of control, and surrender to its power and magic. Without surrender the experience can easily turn into a nightmare. A woman simply and clearly described this predicament when she shared after her second Ayahuasca ceremony that whenever she was in resistance she was in hell, and whenever she was in acceptance she was in heaven.

I consider myself truly blessed because during my very first time drinking Ayahuasca, which I wrote about at the beginning of this book, I was in a situation where I clearly had no control whatsoever over my experience, and the experience itself was the temporary but complete knock out of my rational mind and ego, which are the basic controlling aspects of our being. I was also lucky somehow, because I was too incapacitated in my normal functioning to be able to offer any resistance. All that was left for me to do was surrender. Whenever I was aware enough of the fear I was in, I would breathe deeply, offer my willingness to the medicine, and remind myself that I was safe. Surrendering over and over meant allowing myself to keep being thrust down a cosmic rabbit hole with no apparent end in sight. As scary as the experience was in the moment, it did have a few purposes. The first one was that without disintegration and psychological or ego death, there cannot be any spiritual rebirth. As it happens with most dying processes, this is not necessarily a pretty event, but one that is often met with dread. The second one was equally profound and it was to teach me experientially that I was and am always safe. I had no idea how this medicine would affect me, but I had worked hard on letting go of my fears before the ceremony and was able to offer my trust to Ayahuasca and surrender completely.

I have learned over the years that there is no more beautiful gift we can offer the world than the gift of love and trust. Andean social and spiritual life revolves around the principle of Ayni, i.e., reciprocity. It is this principle that governs all exchanges, all giving and receiving: we receive as much as we are willing to give and vice versa, like some sort of South American yin and yang. We happily return the help received by others when they are in need and gladly mirror Mother Earth's generosity by making her offerings of the sweetest fruit, produce, and flowers. In life, and shamanic work is no exception at all, we receive as much as we are willing to give into any particular activity, process, and relationship.

I had spent most of my life suffering from emotional and spiritual stinginess, never really giving of myself with generosity but rather giving out just enough for fear of being shortchanged. In the same way I realized I had sat in a dark corner waiting to be loved before I would open my heart and love in return. What a misconception! And what a waste! Like many people – and what irony that we should feel this way at a time in history when we enjoy more material goods than ever before! – I have suffered from scarcity issues. I have finally realized that the poverty I was experiencing was of my own doing and stemmed from a belief that there is only a limited amount of resources and love in this world as well as inside myself. If the tenet "all we need is love" has any validity, then, by the principle of Ayni, all we need in order to receive all the love we crave is to love with the utmost abandon and generosity.

The same is true about trust and safety. When we offer our trust to ourselves, to others, to a process such as healing with plant medicine, to God, or what have you, that gift is always appreciated and generously returned. The gift we receive in return for offering our trust is the experience of safety and peace.

My trust in Ayahuasca has been tested a few times since that first time many years ago, but hasn't been broken yet. It is my absolute trust in this medicine that gives me the courage and strength to administer it to other people. I never underestimate its power, but also never doubt its intrinsic benevolence, even when it causes people to go through really challenging and painful moments. Ayahuasca is like a mighty fire that burns away the old and destroys all illusions. As all fires, it needs to be tended with great care and even so, at times its force is too big to be controlled, but once the flames have died out we can see that this devastation is also what creates the necessary conditions for new growth.

When it comes to facing our shadow, we need not only a certain degree of courage, but also and most importantly a willingness to let go of our judgments and see things differently: as long as we consider our shadow as something "negative," it will continue to elude us. Rather, our shadows are simply aspects of ourselves we have denied: fragments of our being that we have, consciously or not, relegated to unconsciousness. By acknowledging and befriending our shadows, we bring them back into the light. Only by accepting and experiencing them fully are we capable of understanding their powerful lessons and integrating them. Integrating what we have disowned makes us whole – literally, it heals us.

There is one main difficulty in this process, and that is letting go of the negative judgments we have attached to these aspects of ourselves: it is our own negative judgment that relegates a certain event or aspect of ourselves into the unconscious. I, for instance, used to hide a lot of myself under layers of shame and denial. As a young Catholic boy I quickly intuited that certain behaviors of mine were far from well-looked upon by the Church and my fellow church-goers, and so I would do my best to hide these aspects of myself from others and myself. The fear of being found out, punished, and cast away turned me into a master of denial. It was only with age that I was able to see these "horrible" and "sinful" parts of myself as simple aspects of myself rather than something to be ashamed of.

A lot of my own personal healing with plant medicines has revolved around self-acceptance, reclaiming aspects of myself I had disowned and denied, letting go of self-judgment, and forgiving myself. To my own surprise, acceptance of my own shadow has eventually paved the way for the genuine acceptance and honoring of my divinity as well, and in the light of such divinity all previous mistakes and perceived shortcomings have been reframed as the simple learning experiences that they were to begin with.

Letting go of judgment can happen only when we become aware and take responsibility for our actions and thoughts, when we take responsibility for the way we feel and live. It is impossible for us to change our world if we keep blaming others for the way it is. Integration happens only with integrity and honesty towards others and oneself. When we have finally let go of all excuses and lies, and have taken responsibility for our lives, guilt disappears. When we are in integrity, our actions, feelings, and thoughts are in alignment with our spirit and the whole Universe – as a result, we no longer fear some hypothetical divine judgment and retribution. We can now relax and see Life for what it really is, unclouded by our own judgments and limiting beliefs.

By stepping beyond the realm of duality of the mind we are finally capable of seeing the shadow with neutrality and a renewed interest – this is the essence of many other spiritual disciplines as well, with the difference that they usually require a much longer time frame. Often people interested in spirituality are unconsciously steeped in duality: they long for what they perceive as the "positive" aspects and rewards of the spiritual path, but are unwilling to embrace their own totality. Many spiritual traditions reinforce this duality with rigid ethical and moral codes, making the journey towards wholeness difficult and tortuous.

Some of the people who have had a fair share of New Age or other kind of spiritual literature and teachings seem to be the most resistant toward acknowledging and embracing their own shadow, in particular their judgments and anger toward themselves and others. They have heard that anger is no solution to their problems and have opted for a numbing of such feelings, a strategy that only reinforces the belief that these patterns and emotions are bad and best avoided altogether. What happens unfortunately is that repressed emotions do not go away and are bound to resurface one way or another, and when they come out after much repression and resistance, it is usually in a rather explosive manner and directed at something or someone that has nothing to do with the real source of our upset.

I personally struggled for forty-five years before I could acknowledge and express the full range of anger and resentment I had secretly harbored against my parents since birth. It took all sorts of workshops and healing work before I could let out and express something that is indeed a taboo in our society. It was a most healing and liberating experience to let out all this rage, and so now I give the permission and gently encourage and support others through the same process whenever I feel that their own judgments prevent them from connecting with all sorts of uncomfortable emotions.

One such occurrence happened a few years ago the first time a friend of mine came to visit me in Peru to drink Ayahuasca. Because of her upbringing this person would rather drown her anger and frustration under generous amounts of alcohol than let her true feelings out. At some point during the ceremony I felt the call to go over and sing a healing song for her. I could feel her struggling to hold her rage, which was right under her skin, so I began to sing with an encouraging tone of my voice and didn't give up on her until she broke down through her resistances and let out a good portion of her anger, which made her feel, needless to say, a lot lighter and better.

Letting go of these human constructs can be a real challenge as so much of who we think we are is invested in them. To make things even more challenging is the fact that modern society has put so much importance into "having" and "doing" that we have forgotten as a collective the value of letting go. We spend our lives not only gathering objects, but also experiences, belief systems, relationships, and emotions, and have forgotten the value of letting go and periodically cleansing our own souls. We all suffer to one degree or another of being psychically anal-retentive.

Healing modalities such as the ingestion of vomit-inducing substances, or enemas, have been virtually removed from Western medicine and are resorted to only in extreme cases. When nothing else seems to work, we make our way to a sweat lodge, an Ayurvedic clinic, or the depth of the Amazon jungle, looking for ways to detoxify our bodies and souls from the debris that clog them.

LETTING GO

As far as I am concerned the most important message that Ayahuasca has for modern men and women is "let go": let go of the social constructs, the psychological armoring, the wounds, and deeply seated traumas that suffocate the spirit and weaken the body.

We are often unwilling to let go as we have so much invested into our identities, even the ones that cause us to be miserable or sick. Our attachment to our wounds and beliefs is extraordinary. Acknowledging to oneself that maybe the choices we have made haven't been the best ones for our own development is no easy thing to do. Sometimes we prefer to stay in our own suffering rather than attempting to change our minds and attitudes.

More often than not, Ayahuasca invites us to let go of emotions, viewpoints, and attitudes that may have been important, perhaps even necessary, for our own physical, emotional, and mental survival and well-being, but that are no longer necessary, truly beneficial, or valid in the present moment. These obstructions actually prevent us from freely and fully experiencing the present moment and stepping lightly into the future. Once again Ayahuasca proves to be an amazing medicine in that it actively supports the letting go process. This is short of miraculous but definitely true according to the experiences of all that have used it. This is its therapeutic effect, its healing quality.

The letting go process under the influence and guidance of Ayahuasca can be as easy or as laborious as one is ready to experience it, depending on one's willingness to go along with the medicine's course of action. When the boundaries created by the ego dissolve, we are able to experience ourselves as a totality rather than a fragmented entity. No longer separated into body, mind, and spirit, we experience who we are and the effects of Ayahuasca multi-dimensionally, as a whole being. The cleansing process happens on all levels, physical, and spiritual, with vomit, defecation, tears, screams, laughter, visions of heavy energies leaving the body or being expelled through the act of vomiting.

It is not unusual for someone to have a clear experience that what one is vomiting isn't simply bile but old conflicts, emotions, or thought patterns. These may take the appearance of dark snakes, spiders, or other insects, but are often clearly perceived to be much more than that. The experience is cathartic and so profoundly inscribed into one's cellular memory and spirit that it becomes simply unforgettable: the psyche has been cleansed and rewired with little chance of permanent amnesia or denial.

It can be painful to reconnect with and feel one's own wounds: unhealed conflicts resurface with all their suppressed energy, not to mention all the judgments and layers of resistance wrapped around them. What was once a simple, if painful, event in one's life has now become an insurmountable obstacle or an evil beast. Facing our wounds is at times nothing short of a heroic fight against one's own darkest forces, where survival is often questioned. Yet, few experiences on this planet can be said to be as rewarding as the healing and letting go of such wounds offered by the drinking of Ayahuasca.

And so it is that after going down the infamous rabbit hole, losing one's mind, and, having no option but to look at our own shadow, we are finally releasing old wounds and heavy energies from the depths of our body and soul. The result of all this is often a feeling of lightness, accompanied by an amazing clarity, increased creativity, and a deep connection to ourselves, others, and the whole Cosmos.

There are multiple levels and degrees of letting go and surrender. Among them I'd like to mention the experience of psychological or symbolical death. I often remind people that drinking Ayahuasca is a wonderful practice for one of the most challenging acts of surrender we are capable of, that of dying. It is remarkable how people with great fear of dying will suddenly find themselves going through this kind of experience during an Ayahuasca ceremony and then later comment on how liberating it was to stop resisting the process and surrender completely and without worries.

CLEANSING THE DOORS OF PERCEPTION

Working with Ayahuasca is like standing in front of a full size mirror. Knowing we are in front of a mirror, we expect it to give us a precise reflection of ourselves, but that mirror is often covered with debris, and as we look at ourselves into that mirror all we see is our wounds and the psychological and mental rubbish amassed there through time. Because we are so identified with our own mental image we believe we are that rubbish and little else. Ayahuasca, at times radically, at times with gentle little swipes, cleanses the mirror so that we are able to get an increasingly clearer picture of who we really are – our own divine nature is finally able to be seen and experienced. Our deepest truths are then revealed to the degree and in the form that we are ready to receive them. All that is needed is to cleanse and prepare our consciousness like a vessel, so that it can hold greater degrees of truth and light.

Just as wise people and spiritual masters have told us throughout the ages, there is no truth to look for out there: we have been carrying it within ourselves all along, and it is only a matter of rediscovering and remembering it. This was my own experience during my shamanic apprenticeship: like countless other people I had been on a spiritual search for many years, reading books, attending workshops, and engaging in various forms of spiritual practice. In the spiritual literature I had often found the notion that everything I was looking for was already within myself, but my search around the world would not stop.

Reading about something and actually having a direct personal experience of it are two totally different things. It was not until my shamanic diet with the Datura plant that I was able to experience first-hand what all of this talk was about. In the first month of my diet with this Plant Teacher I felt how the plant was cleansing me like one would polish a crystal, until it was totally shiny. It was after this process that I realized my whole being had been gently prepared in order to be able to hold greater and greater wisdom, and that such wisdom was not being put inside of me from an outside source, but was actually the resurfacing of a wisdom that had been within me all along. To my great surprise I finally realized what a vast number of spiritual books had been hinting at, and it was amazing to experience the opening of such a rich depository of knowledge and wisdom that had been laying dormant within myself: despite all efforts to the contrary, the spiritual journey is ultimately an inner one.

Ayahuasca is like the best of spiritual teachers in that it doesn't provide yet another set of beliefs, but reconnects us to our own timeless truths. Like the most loving of gurus, this medicine at times makes us cry long and hard but also reflects back to us our own divinity. There is no need for Plant Teachers to fill us with more teachings or dogmas: they know that deep within each living being lies the same loving essence and their main gift to us all is to help us reconnect with such essence. As the psychological and mental lenses of our perception are cleansed, we are finally able to connect with the deeper layers of our hearts and souls. And as the identification with our minds and wounds lessens, we automatically get in touch with our own Higher Self and inner treasures.

In the course of working with Ayahuasca this happens as a result of, and in parallel with, the cleansing and healing process. The image I am fond of using is that of a hot air balloon that lifts up into the stratosphere as sand bags are being released: as we let go of the heavy energies we carry within ourselves, we are capable of regaining altitude, of seeing the whole landscape of our inner and outer lives, and to bask once again in the clarity of Divine Light. This pattern occurs quite frequently during Ayahuasca ceremonies: often there is a descent into the darkest regions of our being, and once the healing and release have been accomplished, we find ourselves in a state of expansion, elation, and often ecstasy. The reconnection to our own light is the source of increased intuition, trust, self-esteem, and the resulting ability to live according to our heart's desire.

"Shadow" and "light" are after all only categories of the mind, and under the effects of Ayahuasca these labels are no longer significant – everything simply *is*. Just as the dualities of the mind are transcended, so are the concepts of time and space: everything happens here and now. In this state of wholeness people often become suddenly clear about deeper layers of who they are, their connection with others, and the Universe. The inner vision, no longer clouded by the illusory drama of life, is reawakened, and the answers one has been looking for are finally visible and clear. It is a powerful and beautiful process that happens effortlessly once we let go of what we have held on for far too long. Just like the cleansing of body and soul, the revelation process happens gradually and can achieve tremendous depth.

Another translation of the word "Ayahuasca" is "Vine of the Soul": by shedding the layers around the psyche we are eventually able to look directly into our souls and understand what our soul path is. We intuit that we are in this world for specific purposes, but those purposes often elude us: we seem to be suffering from some sort of innate amnesia that prevents us from understanding what we came into this world to do. In the Western tradition it is said that an angel erases from our awareness the reasons for our incarnation at the moment of birth. "What am I doing?" and "What am I supposed to do with my life?" These are recurring questions in our lives, particularly to those on a spiritual search. Working with Ayahuasca, the Vine of the Soul, allows people to reconnect with their soul purpose. This may not happen overnight, but it is definitely within the range of what this medicine is capable of catalyzing.

Knowing beyond any doubt what one is here to do gives a totally new flavor to existence: it is an enlightening experience that allows us to clearly focus, direct, and align our thoughts and actions accordingly. This is not to be confused with the search for a career or another way of satiating a demanding spiritual ego. Life choices may become clear, even obvious, but it is only as a result of an increased inner clarity. Actions are taken not to satisfy the ego but to be in alignment with the spirit.

My own personal work with this medicine gifted me with the sudden awareness of my reasons for being in this physical body at this time and on this planet. It was a powerful revelation that has guided me ever since and has given me the coordinates by which I have been making my decisions since. The understanding that my purpose in this life wasn't really that of being successful or important has freed me from the pursuit of things that weren't all that important. Instead I have begun to make choices that were in alignment with my soul path, regardless of social and ego-centered expectations and concerns, and my life has blossomed as a result.

Many people I encounter mention wanting to better know what their life purpose is as one of their main reasons for wanting to drink Ayahuasca. Often their desire goes hand in hand with a wish to be of service to others and make the best possible use of their time, talents, and resources. To those who ask these questions from a place where they feel they have already been wasting enough time in doubt and confusion, I often reply by reminding them that all of us are *always* fulfilling our life purpose already. We may feel discontentment about the general course our life has taken, but that doesn't mean we are wasting our time or doing anything wrong. The fulfillment of one's life contract is not always a happy and straightforward affair. Particularly those on a spiritual path will find their roads winding in often confusing ways and paved with all sorts of challenges. To those suffering from confusion and discouragement in life in general or during a healing process with Ayahuasca I often offer these words by R.L. Stevenson, "It's a better thing to travel hopefully than to arrive." We may find ourselves at a loss from time to time, but can always trust the mysterious roads of our lives to have an important destination.

Part II

"Kai Pacha" by Harry Chavez, 2012

PREPARATIONS FOR
A CEREMONY

Throughout the Americas the main way of spiritual discipline is indissoluble from the concept and practice of purification – purification of the body and the spirit. Sweat lodges, vision quests, the ritual consumption of Peyote, Psilocybin mushrooms, San Pedro cactus, or Ayahuasca: all of these are ways to purify the individual in order to attain a deeper connection to the world of Spirit and Essence. They are cleansing yogas developed over millennia and form the very backbone of Panamerican spirituality. These rituals are not the sole purificatory actions, but are often preceded by various cleansing and other preparatory processes. These measures are very important in order to prepare us, physically and psychologically, and to open us to the work ahead.

Experiencing first-hand the great benefits of a good preparation before drinking Ayahuasca, I am always fairly strict with prospective clients, particularly with habitual consumers of alcohol and other mind-altering substances. The ability of someone to give up such substances for at least a few days before and after working with Ayahuasca is not just a necessary preparatory cleansing but also a test of the psychological fortitude of each participant. If one is not willing or capable of adhering to a few temporary restrictions in order to have this experience, then I believe the person is not quite ready for it yet.

To engage in these deeply affecting practices without the necessary preparation often results in the individual being overwhelmed by the experience and failing to fully benefit from it. Like tantric yoga, the plant medicine path is surrounded by a powerful taboo that is not entirely out of order: this is a very powerful path that can be tricky and sometimes outright dangerous if not engaged in with the most respectful and disciplined attitude.

I often refer to Ayahuasca as "the Ferrari of transformation." Many would love to own and drive a Ferrari but it is statistically proven that the majority of people who drive such a powerful and fast car for the first time end up smashing it not too far from the car dealership. As is the case with certain powerful spiritual practices, the drinking of Ayahuasca also comes shrouded in a thick veil of cautionary tales, which are not entirely out of place. The powerful psychic energies that this medicine ignites are not for the faint of heart, nor for those simply looking for another psychedelic kick.

WHEN AND WHERE

The decision to drink Ayahuasca is rarely a casual one: luckily for us, stories of the extraordinary experiences and healings connected with this medicine are also accompanied by accounts of how challenging those experiences can be. The unpleasantness of the physical reactions of this medicine make it an unlikely candidate as a recreational drug or pastime, and more often than not people approach this medicine only when everything else has failed to bring substantial healing.

When William Burroughs went to South America looking for Ayahuasca, he was very turned off by its effects, which were probably very unpleasant due to his long history of drug abuse. Instead of finding another substance that would provide him with the "ultimate high," he found a medicine that wanted first and foremost to cleanse his body and spirit from all the garbage they were carrying.

For people who have not been raised in close connection with this medicine, it is best to wait until one has reached a certain psychological maturity and stability. In the jungle and among social groups closely connected with this medicine it is not unusual that people start drinking Ayahuasca from an early age, but for the rest of us waiting until adulthood seems to be a more sensible choice.

Because of beliefs or personal preference, many people opt to drink this medicine only in its original birthplace, the Amazon jungle, or only with native medicine people. Many others don't have such an option, and indeed if everybody wishing to drink Ayahuasca nowadays went to the jungle to do so, it would probably result in a serious ecological and social disaster.

Often the connection with the medicine happens in a seemingly casual way, other times one has been searching for it for quite a while until the opportunity to sit in ceremony with it arises. In any way we should always, and that means each and every time, ask ourselves whether the time, the place, and the people connected with the experience are indeed right and conducive to the positive and healing experience we are looking for. Simple availability of the medicine is hardly ever a reason good enough to drink it; having the courage to acknowledge our intuition and say "no" to an opportunity to drink the medicine that doesn't feel 100% right for us is often the wisest of choices. It is important that one feels totally safe and comfortable in order to open oneself up to the medicine. And it is better to get some useful referrals from trustworthy people or the Internet beforehand rather than complaining afterwards about a nightmarish experience. The great diversity of rituals and traditions available today in connection with the use of Ayahuasca should satisfy everybody's wishes and taste: rather than criticizing this or that tradition or shaman, go and find what resonates best with your needs and what works best for you.

When choosing where to drink I believe it is very useful to find a guide who speaks your language or at least someone who can translate with clarity in order to better understand the guide, be able to communicate your experience, and understand whatever feedback you may receive.

Something I have noticed is that people who drink this medicine with a different guide each time seem to benefit less from this process than those who stick with one particular ayahuasquero for more than just one ceremony. I don't believe that one should stay with any single medicine person forever, particularly if one doesn't feel any benefit from doing so; however, there is something to be said about being able to deepen the connection with one healer at a time. In that deepening there is the benefit of increased trust and also the resurfacing of projections and transferences that, when focused upon and owned, can be a source of greater awareness and healing. It is important to keep in mind that whatever healing or spiritual process we engage in is also strongly informed by the healer or spiritual teacher who supports us during such process. Each healer or ayahuasquero carries a different "medicine" (and I don't mean just a different brew but a different energy and different teachings and viewpoints). We feel drawn to this or that healer for very specific reasons: at times the teachings that such relationships bring up are not all that pleasant, but not for that reason are they unimportant. Also, at other times we may feel that this or that ayahuasquero has provided us with everything we needed to receive from them and it is time to move on. Rather than criticizing or resenting them for not being able to take us all the way along our inner journey, we can simply be grateful for their gifts and move on.

Another way to greatly improve the quality of every ceremony is for each participant to spend the day of the ceremony in quiet and keep the following day free of engagements and strenuous activities. It is my belief that an Ayahuasca ceremony begins when we begin our fast and continues until we break our fast the following day. Spending the day of the ceremony in quiet is a good way to leave all stress and nervousness behind, focus on our intentions and gently connect with the medicine. This offering of our time and undivided attention is always appreciated by the medicine and is part of our practice of Ayni, i.e., reciprocity.

If you suffer from some health problem, in particular respiratory and heart conditions (and this is particularly important when drinking Ayahuasca at high altitude), and/or are taking specific medications, it is most important to share that information with the people leading the ceremony well beforehand and discuss with them the suitability of your participation. It is also wise to wait four to six months after important internal surgery before drinking this medicine: the strain on the physical body may actually rip apart sutures and prevent the proper healing after surgery.

DIETARY RECOMMENDATIONS

Traditionally the use of Ayahuasca involves a great deal of preparation, physical and psychological. The guidelines offered here come from the Amazon tradition and ascribing to them is a powerful and effective way of preparing oneself and aligning oneself to an old tradition and its wisdom. These preparations are meant to purify the body and spirit in order to profit from the medicine in the best possible way. Attention is given particularly to food and drink: first and foremost all fermented, acidic/citric and overly ripe foods are avoided – this is to optimize the absorption and effects of the medicine as well as avoid a hypertensive crisis because of excessive amounts of tyramine in the body. As a general rule and to simplify the task, all foods and drinks that need refrigeration (sauces, yogurt, cheeses and so on) are to be avoided as much as possible. Ayahuasca grows in the Amazon jungle, an environment without electricity or kitchen appliances, so it makes sense to prepare for its ingestion by eating foods that don't need refrigeration.

Other foods to be avoided are heavy, oily, and greasy foods that clog the digestive system. A diet consisting of freshly prepared ingredients and light on spices is all that's really needed. Another taboo is the ingestion of pork, traditionally considered by many an impure food, and also because processed pork meat is high in tyramine, which prevents our bodies from assimilating this medicine. Whichever the reason for this taboo, it is a good idea to abstain from it in order to align oneself with a certain belief system and the many generations of Ayahuasca users before us.

Moreover, abstinence from caffeine, alcohol, and recreational drugs is highly recommended. Giving up these substances not only cleanses body and spirit, but also brings up to our conscious awareness all those issues that are buried under the use of intoxicants of all kinds. Drinking Ayahuasca means accessing these unconscious or repressed aspects of our being, and we begin the process beforehand by avoiding the usual ways with which we "medicate" ourselves. Abstaining from these substances is not always easy, particularly because of the uncomfortable situation of feeling things and emotions we have become so proficient at avoiding. By reopening those channels that have become clogged with all sorts of psychic anesthetics, we begin ourselves the healing process.

These days it is often assumed that by simply showing up and paying a fee, any experience is available to us. Ayahuasca, as well as many other traditional rituals, challenges our consumerist attitude and forces us to think about what we actually bring to the ceremony, not just what we want from it. This is a two-way relationship where something is expected from us other than time and money.

In addition to these dietary restrictions, all sorts of cleanses are welcome: the longer and more thorough the preparation, the better and deeper the experience of drinking Ayahuasca.

The cleansing effects of Ayahuasca start on the physical level and later reach the more subtle bodies: by initiating this cleansing process ourselves before the ceremony we facilitate the work of the medicine and allow it to reach deeper layers of our consciousness. This preparation marks the beginning of our relationship with the medicine and allows also for clearer visions during the ceremonies as well as a greater capacity to undergo the process and benefit from it.

Preparation through diet is an important matter but should not become a source of anxiety: freedom is left to the individual to see how to better prepare oneself by using these guidelines. Usually a few days of preparation is enough; in the case of an Ayahuasca retreat involving several ceremonies, two to three weeks of preparation are ideal. The same guidelines are generally followed for just as long after the ceremonies as well: this is a way of inviting the medicine to stay with us long after its ingestion in order to facilitate the integration process.

Despite having been warned of the negative effects of not observing these simple restrictions, I made the mistake of breaking these simple rules right after my second Ayahuasca ceremony and the resulting confusion was all I needed, at least in my own experience, to validate the importance of these guidelines. A woman who worked with me for a few ceremonies, had labeled her visit to Peru as "the beginning of her sobriety" after a couple of years of mild alcohol abuse. After our ceremonies together she went back home and, despite my recommendations, started drinking alcohol again even before her airplane ride to the States and again when aboard the aircraft. By the time she had arrived at Miami airport for her connecting flight she was feeling pretty miserable and nauseous, so much so that she ended up throwing up in one of the airport's bathrooms. To her great surprise all she threw up was the wine she had been ingesting and nothing else.

SEX

Sexual activities, and in general the arousal of sexual energy, are to be refrained from during the same periods of time before and after the ceremonies. This has nothing to do with a repressive view of sexuality, but takes into consideration and with great seriousness the power of sexual energy. By abstaining from sex we are better able to engage in the whole process. Sexuality is an arena that usually comes with a lot of emotional baggage, the kind that is often stirred by the work with Ayahuasca. By avoiding sexual activity we are better able to focus on these issues rather than becoming even more enmeshed with them. Sexual abstinence and refraining from romantic pursuits give us the space and peace of mind necessary to look with clarity into our souls.

By all means it is recommended not to engage, either sexually or romantically, with the shaman in order to avoid all sorts of transference, nsference, and projections. The figure of the ...un is all too often idealized, a phenomenon that people with little integrity are prone to take advantage of. In order to avoid all sorts of problems it is best to simply abstain from such behavior or to wait until the process has been completed. The consequences for people who don't follow this rule are usually very negative because they counteract the benefits of the medicine itself. Of all the instances I have known of where this rule had been broken, there was not one where the people involved, both guides and shamans and their clients, had not suffered greatly from the consequences of their behavior. Shamans often end up, sooner or later, loosing their connection with the medicine and the healing energies they work with as well as the trust of the people they are supposed to help heal and eventually their reputation is rightly damaged for a very long time. Their clients suffer equally by engaging in relationships that are experienced as confusing at best and abusive at worst instead of receiving the healing they deep down long for.

PSYCHOLOGICAL AND MENTAL PREPARATION

Working with Ayahuasca should by no means be taken lightly. The power of this medicine is such that, if unprepared, we risk ending up at the end of the experience worse than when we started. Information is important – and the use of this information is paramount. Reading about the subject and talking to other people who have already drank this medicine is a good starting point and a way to avoid making the same mistakes others have made.

Often the way people are drawn to this medicine is rather serendipitous, at times we come upon it in sudden or mysterious ways. Usually the person who is looking for the kind of healing Ayahuasca has to offer, and is prepared for its medicine, will sooner or later stumble upon it: nowadays Ayahuasca has an interesting way of becoming available to those who need it.

But what do we really mean when we say we want healing? Most people used to contemporary medicine want the pain, whether physical or emotional, to simply and magically stop. Unfortunately these kinds of expectations are fairly unrealistic, and do not take into consideration what healing means and entails. Healing means "becoming whole," not finding a quick fix to one's problems. It involves a process of reawakening to all that we are, including our pains.

We know we want the pain to go away, but are we really willing to go through what is needed in order to heal? Ayahuasca is not an analgesic or a narcotic that makes the pain temporarily go away, actually it is quite the opposite: it forces us to be with and feel our suffering, pains, and fears more intensely than ever, so that we can integrate them.

We tend to be critical of Western medicine and yet, often unconsciously, we approach Ayahuasca with the hope that it will take away all of our pain as if by magic. Over the years of working with this medicine I have come to actually perceive physical pain as a great gift, as a way we communicate to ourselves the presence of a deeper disease. Physical pain is in my opinion just a symptom, and when we embrace it and engage in a dialogue with it, we can actually

91

discover what the real roots of these conditions are. By addressing the roots of our diseases we can actually learn what these conditions are meant to teach us.

Less and less frequently do I perform "extractions" during ceremonies because I believe that if only the symptoms are addressed and dealt with, the person suffering from a certain disease will eventually develop a similar condition until they learn the lessons these diseases are meant to teach them. This is why we seem to attract this or that kind of people, relationships, and situations over and over into our lives: not because we are stupid or cursed, but rather because we are here to fulfill a specific contract with ourselves and until we have learnt this or that lesson we shall keep inviting into our lives the kind of people and experiences that can best help us do so. Our first reaction when someone or something pushes our buttons is often resentment whereas we would do better by being grateful that another opportunity for growth has made its appearance. Maybe this is what is meant by the words "Love thy enemy."

Often people complain of the physical pain they have to endure during the ceremonies and the all-around challenges that the ingestion of this medicine implies. But the physical pain is short-lived despite the fact that it sometimes seems to last for a very long time, while the benefits are long-lasting. A client just recently had an experience where she was shown how time is of little relevance and patience is often the wisest of approaches. However, soon after the end of that same ceremony, she suffered from intense pain in her stomach, which lasted for a couple of hours. In the throes of physical discomfort she quickly forgot the lesson she had just received, and it wasn't until the following morning during our talk together she realized that the importance of patience and the irrelevance of time were not just abstract concepts but something she was being called to practice right away.

So, before drinking Ayahuasca we should ask ourselves how serious we are about engaging in such a challenging process, and how willing we are to surrender to it. Preparing oneself beforehand with some dietary restrictions already reminds one that some important process is at work, and automatically brings to the front certain issues, fears, and doubts. These are often nothing new: just old or forgotten patterns we prefer not to look at but are somehow present in our lives and are now difficult to avoid.

The fears of letting go, of temporarily losing one's mind and control, the prospect of vulnerability, the fear of change that true healing often entails: these are issues that one would do better to examine and make peace with before the actual drinking of Ayahuasca. A long and honest look at one's own inner landscape is the best preparation one can do.

Furthermore, being aware and respectful of one's own limitations is the very beginning of a healthy lifestyle. Peer pressure or a desire to be other than one really is, often prove disastrous to the individual who is not really ready for this medicine. Saying no is often the best thing if in doubt.

The use of Ayahuasca should never be taken lightly or casually, even by the most experienced. Plant Teachers are more than willing to help us whenever we feel the need, just as long as we go to them with the due respect, attitude, and preparation. If we don't, the medicine itself will remind us, often in not-so-gentle ways, of who is really in charge.

Preparing oneself also entails connecting positively with the person who will lead the ceremony and the environment where the medicine will be taken. In order to reach the degree of vulnerability required by working with Ayahuasca it is necessary that one feels relatively safe.

The psychedelic tradition of the 1960's stressed over and over the importance of set and setting, and this is still so today: it makes all the difference between a positive experience and a nightmarish "bad trip." Unfortunately in recent times as more and more people are called to engage with this medicine, our best judgment is often left on the side and we end up in ceremonies with shamans or leaders with little integrity or the necessary preparation to deal with seriously challenging situations. Once again, if either set or setting feels inappropriate, it is better to wait for another occasion.

INTENTIONS AND EXPECTATIONS

A frequently overlooked aspect of this work is the subtle yet radical difference between intention and expectation. The setting of intentions is a very important part of this healing modality as it makes us aware of the reasons we go to Ayahuasca and helps us focus on ourselves and the work ahead.

As we receive as much from this medicine as we are willing to put into the experience, focusing on our intentions is a way of devoting some time and attention to the experience ahead. Preparing our intentions for a ceremony helps us understand the real reasons for approaching this medicine and makes the way for receiving the healing we are longing for.

I used to be fond of telling people that "Ayahuasca doesn't necessarily give us what we want but most importantly what we need." This statement no longer seems to me totally accurate as I now feel that if we approach this medicine with a pure intention, we can trust that whatever happens during any ceremony is somehow in alignment with our intentions. It's just that oftentimes before we can work on themes that are part of our intentions, the medicine invites us to face all the obstacles that prevent us from being truly ready to address the themes of our intentions.

This is often a source of frustration for the ego, which has somehow hoped for and is attached to certain results in unconscious ways. Sometimes we go to Ayahuasca with a desire for certain visions and experiences, but the medicine may point us in a totally different direction, and without much space for bargaining. Such events ought to be dealt with by surrender rather than stubbornness because what we are dealing with is not intention but expectation, and all expectations are a product and an aspect of the ego-mind. When we let go of our expectations we can finally open ourselves to a greater, universal intelligence rarely provided by the limitations of the ego. The medicine has an uncanny ability to know exactly what we need, and we should let her do what she knows best with as little resistance as possible.

At the beginning of a ceremony I ask all participants to offer their intentions to the medicine and the Universe, and then let them go. The medicine may take us right where we wish to go and these intentions may be fulfilled; other times the medicine may see the importance of our intentions but also the need to explore and heal other aspects of our lives before addressing the themes of our intentions. This may happen during one single ceremony or over the course of several.

A woman told me of how towards the end of a ceremony she expressed the wish to explore a certain issue that had been part of her reason for drinking the medicine that night. The answer she got from the medicine was a simple but irrevocable "Not tonight, dear."

Surrendering to the wisdom and healing power of Ayahuasca can be challenging but not impossible: one has simply to acknowledge and remember that the choice one has taken is the right one, that both set and setting are ideal and conducive to allowing oneself a certain degree of vulnerability, and that ultimately one is in safe hands, both those of the medicine and of the people leading the experience.

INTENTIONS PT. 2

Someone recently had the following vision during an Ayahuasca ceremony: *I was climbing a large tree when the spirit of Ayahuasca, under the guise of a giant snake, approached me and said, "If you want to get to the top of this tree, try by beginning your climb at its roots." She then proceeded to swallow me whole so she could take me all the way to the top of the tree by first diving into the earth and then through the roots and the entire trunk of the tree.* When I first heard this story I was struck by its wisdom and accurate description of the healing journey with Ayahuasca.

The healing potential of this medicine is quite astounding, so I always encourage people to go to the very root of their disease. In most cases I believe we suffer from an old spiritual wound of rejection, abandonment, betrayal, humiliation, or injustice.[9] Whereas traditional psychology attributes the reason for our neuroses to childhood traumas, other schools of thought claim that we all come into this life already carrying certain wounds and that our main purpose for incarnating is precisely the healing of such wounds. We therefore seem to pick the most ideal family environment to reactivate these wounds, often choosing parents or ancestral lines that cannily resonate with the issues we came to heal.

One big advantage of such viewpoint is that it helps us shift out of the blaming of others, which, no matter how justified it may seem, has the major disadvantage of keeping us disempowered. Those with a strong victim identity, i.e., prone to blaming others, the environment, society, or God for their misery, are highly encouraged to begin their healing journey by honestly looking at this attitude. The "victim game" has become the most popular game on this planet, to the point that anybody can claim to suffer because of present or long past events and abuses. There are so many individuals and ethnic groups claiming their victim title that we are running out of people who can actually help these victims since everyone else is a victim too.

A victim attitude often gives also rise to unreasonable feelings of entitlement. Because we believe that our pain is somebody else's fault, like something hurtful has been done to us, we feel entitled to some special treatment from others or the Universe, including

9   I am deeply grateful to Lise Bourbeau and her book *Heal Your Wounds and Find Your True Self* for the insights regarding these basic soul wounds.

Ayahuasca. As somebody discovered during a recent ceremony, the Universe doesn't owe us anything, but we owe everything to the Universe. Holding on to feelings of entitlement is a way of holding on to expectations that are bound to cause disillusionment and disappointment. Humility and patience on the other hand are virtues whose importance in this work cannot be stressed often enough.

There is an infinite variety of dramatic stories, but they can all be summarized in stories of rejection, abandonment, humiliation, betrayal, and injustice, and all these stories are ways for us to hold on to the belief and experience that we are separate from Divine Source as well as others. Our "stories" or "personal dramas" are dramatic devices that can be used to either convince ourselves that we are less than our true Divine Self, or as a teaching device meant to help us remember our essential divinity. The difference lies in our attitude toward the challenges of life.

On the one hand we intuit that we are fundamentally different than what we create ourselves as, and that despite our best intentions and grandiose plans, we always find ourselves falling short of manifesting our full potential. On the other hand we hold on to all sorts of limiting beliefs and judgments that keep us small and disempowered, not to mention the fact that we spend a lot of our time rehashing in our minds painful events that are long gone or worrying about a future that doesn't truly exist.

It was upon reading Lise Bourbeau's book years ago that I realized that the constellation of patterns I kept acting out in my life were characteristic of a wound of abandonment, rejection, and betrayal. I embarked on this healing journey with hope and the determination to eventually be able to let go of a story that kept me feeling afraid of true intimacy and ultimately unloved. Because of immigration laws in Switzerland in the 1960's and the resulting need to hold a job in order to legally stay there, my parents had apparently no other choice but to put me in a nursery right after birth. Plant medicines were instrumental in helping me connect with the pain of isolation, confusion, and abandonment experienced as a baby, which I had had until then little recollection of. After many ceremonies and much inner work I finally succeeded in letting go of the urge to blame my parents for the traumatic experience of spending the first year of my life in a children's clinic. Letting go of blame helped me connect with my own experience rather than disowning it, and eventually I understood that I had chosen the circumstances of my birth for the specific reason of healing my soul wounds of rejection and abandonment. This not only allowed me to offer my parents my heartfelt forgiveness, but also lead to feeling deep gratitude towards them for being part of my healing process.

It's interesting how, due to the plant medicine work I lead on my land and the resulting energetic presence of both Ayahuasca and San Pedro, I seem to be benefiting from these medicines without necessarily ingesting them. This is actually a rather common experience shared by many who feel the benevolent influence and presence of these healing energies even years after their last ceremony. A friend did not only hear the spirit of Ayahuasca speak to her incessantly on her flight back to Europe after visiting me, but has received regular visits since and feels that this energy is always with her, guiding and supporting her.

Connecting with the full spectrum and core of my emotional and spiritual pain has by no means been a linear experience and, just like everybody else, I have had moments of total confusion and discouragement, particularly when I realized that patterns I thought I had dealt with would resurface in all their stubborn glory. One of the most important, and humbling, spiritual lessons I have had to learn and practice since moving to Peru has been patience. It is said all along the Andes that patience is the science of peace and never have I felt more foolish in my life than each time I have lost my patience in this country.

In patience there is also an element of trust and intuitive knowing that one is on the right path. I believe that complete healing and enlightenment is not only available to us all but also ultimately inevitable. To me the vision of Heaven is not complete without each and everyone of us in it. Gautama Buddha is quoted as saying that once we hear of enlightenment, we will not stop our search until we have found what we have been looking for. I understand this to mean that ultimately this is already a done deal and that we are all bound to find what we are looking for, i.e., eternal happiness and union with the Divine. So it's really just a matter of time (and time matters little when compared to eternity), or rather it's a matter of how long we are wanting to keep ourselves in suffering and pain and what we are willing to do to get ourselves out of this predicament.

Honestly I must say that the peeling of the several layers of my own inner onion as I went through the different aspects of my wounds of abandonment and betrayal has not been an easy affair. Finally connecting with the deep rage and pain I had been holding inside was a heroic feat. My fears would tell me I would never get to the bottom of it, and unconsciously I was also afraid that feeling such pain would kill me. As I laid in agony in my garden one night after much screaming, what I experienced was indeed a little death or rather the amazing inner quiet that follows the release of long-held pain.

The journey isn't over but years after its beginning I feel I have fulfilled my own personal soul contract with myself. Thanks to plant medicines - and a long list of other teachers and spiritual practices - I have been able to achieve spiritually what I sure longed for but never felt was truly possible nor available to me in this lifetime. The inner peace and love I feel in my heart as well as the general positive attitude that permeates all aspects of my life are the tangible results of years of fruitful letting go. As I mentioned earlier, ultimately what I needed to let go of was the story that kept me feeling unloved. Once I did let it go I could finally experience the deeper truth of ever-present Divine Love.

Perfect peace is a difficult state to maintain on this planet but also no longer an absolute priority now that I have tasted it and know that peace to be my natural state and birthright beyond the illusions of this world. I marvel at my own journey and feel totally blessed by the gifts of healing and spiritual awareness I have received throughout the years by Mother Earth in general, and Ayahuasca in particular.

INTENTIONS AND EXPECTATIONS: THE DANCE BETWEEN SURRENDER AND ACTIVE PARTICIPATION IN THE PROCESS OF DRINKING AYAHUASCA

In my work with people drinking Ayahuasca I always recommend taking some time before each ceremony to feel what one wishes to receive from this medicine. This is a way to initiate the process and to focus on what themes one wishes to address or be addressed during the ceremony and it helps figure out what exactly are the reasons for engaging with this medicine and how to best go about it. As I said earlier, before one drinks I ask everybody to offer those intentions to the medicine and the Universe and then let them go and see what happens. My recommendation is to bring up those intentions again during the ceremony and to start exploring them with the help of the medicine only in the case they haven't yet been addressed, and when the effects are no longer as strong and there is nothing else going on in one's experience, but always without any expectation that our intentions may be fulfilled.

Drinking Ayahuasca is foremost an exercise in surrender and acceptance to what the medicine has to offer, but at times it also asks for our active participation in the process. The dance between surrender and active engagement is often an intricate but not impossible one. What is most painful for me in my work is seeing people getting upset and frustrated because to their eyes "nothing happened" or their intentions weren't addressed. Attachment to the fulfillment of our intentions and the resulting anger or disappointment is a sign that the mind is subtly at work and that an element of unconscious expectation has crept into the experience. When addressed with calm and awareness, one can often identify in such occurrences very familiar patterns such as self-sabotage, the tendency to set for oneself unrealistic goals, or the wish to overlook some basic psychological issues that nevertheless end up showing up in our experience whether we like it or not.

At one end of the spectrum are often childhood issues of projected expectations and the anger and disappointment for failing to meet them, which in most cases results in deep anxiety and feelings of unworthiness. At the other end we find people who have had a history of drug use that was meant to help them escape and avoid feeling certain things. They may turn to Ayahuasca with the hope of finally addressing those issues but in their consciousness they still hold the pattern "altered states = escape." In those cases then I have witnessed how the medicine, which is intrinsically a consciousness-altering one, has often no psychoactive effect at all. Traditionally in the jungle this scenario is explained as the conflictive presence of the spirit of Substance (or Plant) X and the spirit of Ayahuasca. In my opinion, another way of explaining this is that apparently "the medicine is not working" but truly what it is doing is force the individual to break the escapist pattern and deal with their issues in a state of almost complete sobriety.

As we can see, the results of ingesting this medicine, whether we like them or not, always point to unresolved issues that need addressing and letting go as part of the healing and transformation process.

FROM THE BOTTOM UP

Ayahuasca often works its purificatory magic starting from the densest, i.e., physical, to the subtlest levels of our being. I have witnessed many people having to go through intense physical purging before they could receive any insight or vision from this medicine.

When a dear friend visited me in the jungle some years ago, she had just sobered up after a second bout of drug addiction. As a result she sat through two ceremonies that involved only intense vomiting and defecating. She was also on a cleansing diet with the plant Ajo Sacha (*Mansoa Allinacea*) and fully aware of the toxicity she had been collecting in her body. Still, it was hard for her to endure the hunger, the mosquitoes, and the purging without any mind-expansion whatsoever. On the third ceremony Don Francisco sang a special icaro into my friend's medicine and by the end of the ceremony we had a new convert: the medicine had finally spoken to my friend in all her glorious wisdom, which stopped my friend's whining and complaining altogether.

For years she kept going to the medicine asking for physical cleansing until I suggested to her that maybe it was time for her to ask Ayahuasca for some deeper healing and that's when she began a long and powerful process of healing the pain of a particularly abusive relationship that had left her scarred, fearful, and with a very low self-esteem, and which had been one of the reasons for her past drug abuse. It was a blessing to see her once again in the same temple in the jungle five years after her first Ayahuasca experience and finally dealing with the emotional pain she had so skillfully hidden from herself for many years.

So, one way to "climb the wisdom tree" of Ayahuasca can be by asking the medicine first for physical, then emotional, mental, and eventually spiritual healing. These levels are of course all entwined and truly part of a whole, but this is as good a route as any. Another way of focusing our intentions is by using the chakra system as a reference. I have met some skilled mediums and healers who had never before truly dealt with mommy and daddy and, despite their talents, one could sense how shaky their emotional and mental foundations were. If one is interested in building a solid house, the placing of its cornerstones need all our care and attention. So, before we approach the medicine asking for an open heart or the opening of the third eye, we would do well to ask ourselves if there are other lower charkas issues that need healing first.

These issues can be:

- self-sabotaging patterns and victim identity,
- unworthiness,
- survival and scarcity issues,
- fear of death and the resulting control mechanisms,
- compulsive and obsessive behaviors,
- sexual and body shame,
- sexual and gender identity issues,
- emotional issues connected with our parents and family environment,
- self-esteem and trust issues,
- criticism against others or ourselves,
- power struggles with people of the same or opposite sex,
- themes connected with our gender, ethnic roots, religious and cultural backgrounds, and ancestral lines.

Even if we don't address these issues directly, we can trust the medicine to bring them up to our attention sooner or later, one way or another. This was the case of a man who finally came to visit me in Peru for two months. I was actually dumbfounded when he told me after our first ceremony together that he had had Ayahuasca sixty times beforehand in his native country. The reason for my surprise was that before me was a man who had clearly not dealt yet in his work with the medicine or otherwise with some basic fears and emotional issues. At the root of his successful escapist patterns there seemed to be some deeply ingrained self-loathing, which was so strong it kept him miserable but also safe from any meaningful self-examination. It was clear that we had to start from the beginning, which meant for him the slow and painstaking process of facing all these aspects of himself that he had run away from his entire life. Despite his intuition that working with Ayahuasca in Peru was going to be a whole different story, he sure didn't expect the larger-than-life and impossible to avoid mirror the medicine kept holding up to his face ceremony after ceremony. It was a difficult process but even he was finally willing to admit months later that the work we had done together had been much needed and very helpful.

Yet another meaningful way of working on our intentions, and this is particularly helpful in the case of a series of ceremonies, is by simply observing what is coming up for us, either physically or otherwise, after each ceremony and taking these signs as indicators of what needs to happen next in our process. Because of this I always like to talk to each participant before each ceremony to see where they're at and see if perhaps there are overlooked signs or reactions that may point to important issues that could benefit their attention.

An example of this happened recently with a young couple from Europe who did a two-week "dieta" under my supervision. On the morning before our last ceremony together, the young woman, who had suffered from episodes of vaginal dysplasia, shared with me that that morning she was feeling pain in the area of her left ovary. We had addressed the emotional components of her recurring illnesses and so that morning I told her that I felt it was time for her to ask for physical healing as well if she wanted to. That night a long series of entities came one by one to perform physical healings on her reproductive organs and by the end of the night she felt healed and saw herself as a mother with child. Her boyfriend on the other hand spoke to me that morning of the "downs" he had been experiencing after each ceremony and his ways of dealing with the ensuing restlessness and upset. There was something that he was running away from and even though he had repeatedly put the intention before each ceremony to connect with this resisted experience, little progress had been made. My suggestion was for him to connect with the fear associated with eluding this pain and to contemplate without judgment the ways in which he runs away from himself. This helped a great deal in encouraging him to look in earnest at his life and the ways in which he distracts himself in order (not) to deal with himself.

LAST BUT NOT LEAST

I believe there is great power in asking specifically for what we want and need. This is one of the reasons why I ask people to spend as much time as possible focusing on their intentions before each ceremony and to put these intentions into the medicine before they drink Ayahuasca. I also ask people to let these intentions go as soon as they have been offered and to simply relax and let the medicine take them wherever they need to go. My suggestion is to hold such intentions as lightly as possible, without attachment.

One situation where I feel it can be appropriate to gently ask the medicine to shift gears by reminding her of our intentions is when we get stuck for a very long time in a whimsical fun fair scenario that doesn't seem to be particularly meaningful. In such cases we can thank the medicine for such visions and also ask her if it is possible to explore other themes closer to our hearts. The other time that I see suitable to remind the medicine of our intentions is when we are no longer in the throes of the medicine and yet still benefitting from its consciousness-expanding effects. Of course, in both cases, we should be open to whatever response our requests get.

When talking about intentions, the most common question I hear is whether it is enough to simply be open to receive whatever is in store for us at this time. My answer is, "Yes, of course!" One shouldn't be shy to express to the medicine one's willingness to surrender completely to her healing care if one feels it's appropriate and beneficial.

Finally, when it comes to formulating our intentions, my recommendation is to feel what may be the cause of a particular imbalance or disease and to ask the medicine to help us connect with it, embrace it, and learn from it everything we have failed to learn so far, and, ultimately to support us in letting it go. For instance our goal may be to open our hearts. Upon closer inspection we may feel that our judgment of others is our main obstacle to keeping an open heart. In this case then we could ask the medicine to help us deal with our excessive criticism. In the case of wishing for better health, one could ask the medicine to remove not just all toxins, but also toxic emotions and thought patterns that prevent the physical body from functioning optimally. Here is a short list of intentions that have greatly benefited me in the past:

- Show me what I'd rather not look at.
- Show me the game I am playing with myself (or others).
- May you enter those places of my being that I haven't yet trusted you to visit and help me heal.
- Help me become aware and let go of those unconscious resistances and limiting beliefs that keep me small and in the past.
- Help me own my own projections.
- Do me, I'm all yours.

PERSONAL AND INTERPERSONAL DYNAMICS DURING A CEREMONY

Certain inner dynamics are likely to resurface during an Ayahuasca ceremony – among them fear, frustration, and lessening of self-esteem: these are often perceived with annoyance and reacted to harshly, whereas it is the very work of the medicine that brings back to the surface these feelings so that we can become aware of them and heal them. At the source of these feelings we often find unmet expectations, either from others or ourselves, and at the source of these expectations we find an ego out on the loose and screaming for attention, which is why expectations are best left at the door before an Ayahuasca ceremony.

It is also important not to compare one's own experience with that of others: each one of us has a unique makeup and is on a specific place on our spiritual path. Therefore, it is better to acknowledge our own uniqueness rather than wishing for a different experience. Comparing oneself to others and wishing we experienced what others have is ultimately a way of self-sabotage and unkindness toward oneself. Fully embracing and appreciating who we are in every moment of our lives is one of the goals of healing, and the sooner we start the better.

When I first started leading Ayahuasca ceremonies I would often hear from my clients of visions, the magnificence of which I myself had never experienced, so much so that I started feeling a bit of envy. It took me a while before I acknowledged such feelings and a little longer before I would let go of this game against myself so that I could listen and rejoice without jealousy. Fully accepting my own experiences with the medicine without wishing they were any different than what they were or wishing they were as or more profound and colorful than those of others was a true blessing.

THE CEREMONY

A yahuasca ceremonies traditionally take place at night and in darkness – some shamans even refrain from drinking during full moon nights because they say light interferes with the visions.

People taking part in the ceremony usually do so on an empty stomach: the emptier the stomach, the deeper the cleansing. When I first started my apprenticeship, the medicine told me right away not to bother with the light lunch that used to be served at Sachamama. Years later I discovered that now Don Francisco no longer offers lunch on ceremony day. Some exception may be made for people with hypoglycemia or those with a tendency to develop too much acidity in their stomach when fasting. A light snack in the middle of the day is usually all that is needed in such cases.

The fast should be observed until the following morning but again an exception can be made for those who need to take some medication before they go to sleep. Provided that there is no conflicting interaction between Ayahuasca and any other medication, it is always best to take the latter as much time apart from the ingestion of Ayahuasca as possible.

Individual buckets or a place for vomiting are provided, as well as nearby toilets. During the ceremony participants usually sit or lay down, whichever is more comfortable, and are expected to move as little as possible so as not to disturb the ceremony and others in attendance. Often people have a tendency to slouch or lay down when in the throes of Ayahuasca, but it is often preferable to remain seated with a straight spine as this position actually facilitates the work and the movement of energies. Lying down in the hope of lessening the effects of the medicine is unfortunately counteractive most of the time. On the other hand, in the case of people with a strong mind and a tendency to want to stay in control, I am the first one to recommend that they lay down in a supine position in order to facilitate an attitude of surrender. A dignified posture is always appreciated in a ceremony but ultimately comfort and a posture, both physical and mental, conducive to letting go are in my opinion more important.

As sources of light are often a distraction, people are asked to keep the use of artificial lights such as flashlights to a minimum. The mindful use of flashlights and lighters can easily make the difference between a smooth and a chaotic ceremony.

Ayahuasca ceremonies are shared experiences where each individual is asked to hold their space, physically as well as psychically. First and foremost, people attending a ceremony should refrain from speaking to each other during the whole course of the ceremony. Secondly, there are people specifically designated and trained to take care of those who drink, so that the participants can focus exclusively on their own experience. At times the emotional reactions of some participants bring out some co-dependent behaviors, such as the need to comfort or generally help the other person. Despite the good intentions, this is often a way for the person wanting to offer help to distract oneself from their own issues, or simply the manifestation of unconscious behaviors. If such reactions arise it is best to simply notice them and then return our attention inwards.

Ayahuasca shows us the illusory dramas of our lives, and its work is to shatter those illusions. When we try to comfort others, what we often end up doing is reinforcing those dramas and making them even more real. It is for this reason that people are expected to refrain from giving any unsolicited help, unless the person leading the ceremony asks for it specifically. When discussing this important aspect, I always remind people that what they may project and perceive as something painful and needing their attention, such as someone's crying or screaming, may be the very best thing that ever happened to the person experiencing it and a great source of healing. Personally I have an absolute trust in this medicine, therefore I always assume that whatever happens to the people drinking it under my guidance is benefitting them, no matter how painful the experience may seem to the untrained eye. Rather than trying to end their suffering altogether, I remind them that they are safe and encourage them to embrace whatever they are experiencing.

A woman once became very scared at the very beginning of her first Ayahuasca ceremony. I gently held her hand and instead of telling her that there was nothing to fear, I encouraged her to feel the fear that the medicine was bringing up for her. I stayed with her and reminded her to simply breathe while feeling this deeply-held fear until she came out of it, not by avoiding it but by going through it. It was a very liberating and empowering experience for her.

PHYSICAL AND EMOTIONAL RELEASES

Drinking Ayahuasca causes all sorts of releases, physical, and spiritual: there may be vomiting, defecating, spitting, uncontrollable body movements, crying, shouting, laughing, singing, and so on. All these reactions to the medicine should not be in any way controlled or repressed: it is precisely this sort of release that comes with healing. Ayahuasca cleanses the body and spirit of all those energies that are no longer beneficial to us, and that prevent us from fully becoming who we are. So these releases are to be welcomed and not resisted.

A lot of people have a deep-seated aversion to vomiting and involuntary bowel movements. Unfortunately there are no ways of avoiding them, and one should accept and appreciate them as simply part of the work, actually as an important part of the work because they are expressions of the medicine working. In the English language people use the expression "getting sick" when they refer to the act of vomiting, and often people associate vomiting with past experiences of food poisoning or alcohol and drug abuse when the body actually tried to get rid of toxicity and heal itself. I often remind people that when they feel nauseous and about to vomit, they are not "getting sick": they are actually "getting better" by letting go of toxins and heavy thoughts and emotions.

Vomiting is not an absolute necessity and there are some people who never purge this way. If, for whatever reason, someone is unable or unwilling to vomit but sense that the medicine is inviting them to do so, they should let the ceremony leader know because this means in many cases that the person will remain under the effects of the medicine much longer than usual. At other times people put up a struggle against the medicine: they decide it is time for the medicine to come out of their system and do everything in their power to expel it, often without any success. Once again we need to remind ourselves of the intelligence of this medicine and allow it to do its work in its own time rather than upon demand or according to our mind's time: the rhythm of Nature is often slower than our egos wish. This is often a humbling but deeply enriching discovery.

A friend would often hit a particular aspect of herself that made her feel very uncomfortable during ceremonies. This experience was often paired with heavy nausea. Over and over she would try to induce vomiting but without success and then proceed to spend the rest of the ceremony feeling defeat and failure. Then, one night, once she was back in her bed after the ceremony had ended, she gave up the fight and accepted the nausea as part of her process. To her great surprise she was suddenly enveloped by a very sweet and nurturing energy and spent the rest of the night making beautiful sounds with her voice while the invitation on the part of the medicine to stop trying so hard kept echoing in her mind.

The strongest effects of the medicine usually occur at the beginning of the ceremony, once the medicine has entered our system and starts to affect our bodies and consciousness. The effects of the alteration can be so dramatic that one can react with fear and panic, and often wishes for the experience to magically stop: this is a somewhat unreasonable expectation and one is advised to simply go with the flow. I always warn those who drink Ayahuasca with me for the first time that the one thing I cannot do is make the effects of the medicine stop, which is why I always prefer to be on the safe and cautious side when giving out the medicine to people who haven't sat with me in ceremony before. We can always drink more later on if we wish but won't be able to backtrack once the medicine is already in our system.

In the case of a strong reaction to the medicine, the best attitude is one of surrender and patience: the medicine and the person drinking it have an unwritten contract to fulfill, and it isn't until the completion of that contract that the medicine is going to let go and stop its work.

Emotional release is welcome and part of the purification process. Take your time to feel and express however necessary those emotions as healthily and wholeheartedly as you can, without self-judgment or self-consciousness. To me Ayahuasca ceremonies are not a performance, but if anything an opportunity to let go of our perceived need to perform and prove something, either to ourselves or to others.

As mentioned before, the release of old heavy energies is sometimes accompanied by visions of these energies actually leaving the body and spirit. Either way these releases are deeply felt and cathartic, and the more genuinely these releases are welcomed and expressed, the deeper their benefits.

DRINKING AYAHUASCA

At the beginning of a ceremony, after whatever preliminaries the ceremony leader is using – these usually involve the blowing of tobacco smoke to purify the participants and the blessing of the ceremonial space and medicine through prayer and song - each participant is finally summoned to drink the brew. While holding the cup, it is helpful to put one's intentions into it before drinking its contents. Ayahuasca is a notoriously foul-tasting brew, and it is recommended to drink it as quickly as possible, without breathing through the nose. But it is very important that while we try and get as little taste of it as possible, we also make a space in our physical body as well as spirit, where this medicine can stay and do its work. My recommendation, particularly to those who are reluctant and concerned from the very beginning, is to drink the medicine with a big "Yes" in their hearts and minds. On the one hand the medicine needs to stay in the stomach for at least 15 to 20 minutes in order to take effect, on the other, without our openness of heart and mind, the medicine will have trouble working as intended.

The effects of the medicine vary greatly from brew to brew, but also from ceremony to ceremony, mainly because we are different, in a different state of mind, and with different intentions each time we drink it. This is why it is basically impossible to predict how one ceremony will unfold, or how one will be affected by the medicine. Even experienced drinkers of Ayahuasca are often surprised by the different experiences they have with the same brew and within a short period of time. All mental scenarios are then best left behind while the awareness is focused on what is actually happening in the moment.

In most cases the participant is allowed later on to drink more if needed or wished. This is left to the participant's discretion – it is generally assumed that one is wise enough to know one's own limits and respect them. Contrary to some widely publicized misinformation about the use of entheogens, one doesn't drink Ayahuasca to "get high": this is not a competition to see how much one can drink and withstand. It is not a matter of drinking oneself into oblivion but drinking just enough for the medicine to make its way into our beings and do its work. The goal in my opinion is the deliberate and careful opening and expansion of consciousness. The consequence for those who drink more Ayahuasca than they can handle is often a confused and seemingly endless tour de force with little benefit. Terence McKenna coined and popularized the expression "heroic dose" when talking about the ingestion of large amounts of Psilocybin mushrooms. Unfortunately there is nothing heroic about drinking more Ayahuasca than one can handle. The experience can feel like intense poisoning or overload. When it did happen to me once I had the clear feeling that my nervous system was being flooded with more neurotransmitters than I could handle; the result was suffering from the worst and most intense headache for a full hour and not being able to do anything about it except wait it out and hope my brain wouldn't short-circuit. Of course it didn't, but in that long hour it felt like a distinct possibility.

There is a simple and easy way of determining whether one needs to drink more or not: if sixty minutes after drinking you find yourself wondering whether you have had enough, that means you probably haven't. After that it is up to you to decide whether you actually want to drink more. I personally encourage people to make this little extra effort and drink enough to enter fully the space of the medicine rather than standing on its doorway. Perhaps due to its unpleasant taste but more often because they fear that something is wrong with them, some people complain about the fact that they need to drink more than others, but it is really quite irrelevant how much one has to drink provided that one has had enough and not too much, and you will be glad you did.

ICAROS

Ayahuasca ceremonies make extensive use of the universal power of sound for healing and the work with consciousness. Many cultures have developed over millennia a deep science of sound and music, and this is particularly evident in shamanic, religious, and mystical traditions. In the Indian or Taoist traditions, the science of mantras has been developed and applied extensively for healing purposes; drumming and singing are an essential part of North American shamanic journeys. The list of examples could go on indefinitely.

Humans the world over have since ancient times discovered how powerfully sound affects consciousness, and as a result the physical body as well. As the subtlest of our senses of perception, hearing is the one that most directly affects our spirit, a fact that has not escaped the pioneers of consciousness exploration. Music, drumming, chanting, singing, and praying, are all very important aspects of shamanic work. Since the 1960's, we have witnessed an important resurgence in the West of music with a strong rhythmic content, and the psychedelic revolution has been instrumental in the creation of large amounts of music specifically designed to enhance altered states of consciousness. This is evident in contemporary dance electronic music, the phenomenon of world music, and various movements of trance dancing.

By using different rhythm patterns, scales, and melodies, we are capable of altering our moods and spirits, and elicit particular emotional responses. The power of music can be used alone, as in meditation or shamanic journeys, with dancing, or synergistically with mind-altering substances, whereby the effects of such substances are enhanced by the music. All of these are options left to the taste and preference of the individual, and appear in various guises among different cultures.

In Amazonian shamanism, song and music are used in all aspects of ritual work and ceremonies. The songs that are integral part of an Ayahuasca ceremony are known as "icaros." They are sung either alone (a cappella) or accompanied with musical instruments, most common of all a "shacapa," which is made of a bundle of dry elongated leaves. Icaros are sung to bless the medicine and to accompany the participants through all the stages of the ceremony: there are icaros to open the ceremony and protect the space and participants, to activate the medicine and amplify or lessen its effects, icaros for healing, and icaros to call specific energies and spirits.

A ceremony without icaros is quite like a symphony where half the instruments are left silent. Icaros are the essential tool used to enhance the effects of the medicine and guide the participants through the experience. As a friend once put it: they are the little boat that helps the participants cross the sometimes choppy waters of Ayahuasca ceremonies.

Shamans use icaros deliberately to affect the experience of the participants, well aware of the amplified effects sound has on their altered states of consciousness. It is a synergy in that Ayahuasca and the icaros are used complementarily: sound enhances the effects of the medicine, and Ayahuasca opens the consciousness to a degree where sound becomes an effective healing tool, capable of rearranging energy patterns, from the atomic and physical to the subtle levels of the soul and spirit. Among Shipibo Indians for instance, illness is perceived as a disruption of these energy patterns, which are visible to the shamans under the effects of Ayahuasca and have become the main source of inspiration for their weavings and art. By singing certain icaros these shamans effectively sing these patterns back into order and harmony. Through the use of the fine, vibratory quality of sound, healers are capable of bringing healing to the body and soul without surgery or medications. Sound is their medicine, and the use and mastery of icaros are the signs of an accomplished ayahuasquero.

Icaros are handed down from shaman to shaman, part of their cultural lore and science, but they are also directly transmitted to humans from the spirit realm. Songs are given by the plants themselves or by other spiritual entities in the same way we receive messages through non-ordinary means of communication, visions or intuitions. Just like in the West African and Afro-Brazilian religions, Amazonian medicine people are aware of the specific vibratory patterns and sound signatures characteristic of different spiritual entities and forces, and they use these particular sounds and rhythms to summon their corresponding energies. Each Plant Teacher or spirit doctor has its own songs, and by singing their icaros their presence and help in the healing work is invoked. Actually, the song is in itself a manifestation of that energy or spirit, and its qualities are deliberately used according to the needs of the participants.

In the same way that Ayahuasca has a particular vibration and quality that supports cleansing and letting go, other plants and spirits have their own identities and powers: some are nurturing, some are helpful with one condition or another, some are toxic, and so on. The principle is similar to homeopathy but taken to its extreme and logical conclusion: the vibration of any particular medicine is what really matters and affects most effectively consciousness and its physical manifestations. This aspect of shamanic healing is sometimes difficult for the rational Western mind to grasp. Fortunately it does not need to be fully understood in order to benefit from it: all we need to do is maintain an open attitude and embrace with trust a somewhat mysterious way of interacting with the world. Everybody is touched by the music and songs performed during a ceremony. In most cases participants are welcome to sing once the ceremony is well under way. It's important for participants to be aware that taking too much space with their singing, vocalizing, or constant humming may be distracting or unnerving to others and possibly a source of resentment and conflict. Not monopolizing everyone's attention with our enthusiastic but perhaps not entirely welcome carrying-ons ensures the smooth and peaceful unfolding of a ceremony.

I was actually kicked out of a ceremony once and put somewhere else where I wouldn't disturb anyone. I was totally unaware and unable to control my voice, which kept erupting into quite elaborate but totally out of place singing. When asked by the ceremony leader or other participants to lower our singing or stop it altogether, it is a sign of maturity and responsible behavior to follow such requests without question. That we are being asked to be quiet means there are probably plenty of good reasons to do so and it is not up to us to challenge such request and not honor it.

Most of us already have or will find ourselves sitting in a ceremony next to someone whose behavior we find distracting or annoying. I have been told to shut up and I have told others to please tone it down. When it was clear that my request wouldn't be fulfilled, there have been times when I would leave the space altogether until it got quieter. In those instances it seemed easier and more effective to distance myself from the source of my distraction than to get into a discussion about it. Still, I think it is appropriate to kindly ask others for quiet; it is just not very realistic to expect people who are in an altered state of consciousness to always honor our wishes and needs.

TOBACCO

Jungle Tobacco (*Nicotiana Rustica*), a native plant of the Americas, is not to be confused with the kind of tobacco more commonly found around the world today (*Nicotiana Tabacum*). Not only is its nicotine content much higher, but it is chemically more complex and potentially mind-altering, and is extensively used in Amazonian shamanism and Ayahuasca ceremonies. Its purifying and cleansing qualities are powerful accessories in the work with Ayahuasca, to the point of being also a common additive to the Ayahuasca brew itself.

The blowing of smoke is used to bless the medicine and other ritual objects. Participants often have Tobacco blown on them, most often on the crown chakra and the hands, at the beginning of the ceremony, and later on to further cleanse or open clogged channels of the individuals who need it or may benefit from it. Ready-made cigarettes of this kind of Tobacco are found in markets all over Peru and are called "mapachos."

The energy of Tobacco is helpful to induce vomiting when participants feel a strong need to throw up but have difficulty doing so. Last but not least, Tobacco is used to clear and open up the mind in order to connect with Spirit.

These days Tobacco has become, perhaps due to its easy availability in urban areas, a popular healing and diagnostic tool in its own right. Shamans specializing in its use are known as "tabaqueros," and are often called for cases of physical illness or witchcraft.

AGUA DE FLORIDA AND PERFUMES

Together with hearing, smell is the other truly subtle sense of perception, capable of affecting human consciousness and psyche in powerful ways. Agua de Florida, manufactured by Lanman & Kemp – Barclay & Co., is a commercially available perfume that is used in practically all non-Christian spiritual and shamanic traditions of South and Central America, from Brazilian Candomblé to Amazonian and Andean shamanism, all the way to Cuban Santeria. Like Tobacco, it is used for purification and blessing.

Another use for this cologne, typical of Peruvian shamanism, is the extraction of heavy energies from individuals. The process is called "chupar" (literally, "to suck out"), and is performed by the shaman during ceremonies by holding a small quantity of the perfume in his or her mouth and sucking out the other person's stuck energies or illness. The perfume is immediately spat out after the procedure together with the energies just sucked out. "Chupadas" can be performed in a variety of ways depending on the healer's tradition and style, and also using other perfumes as well.

Perfumes contain the essence and energy of flowers, which, just like plants, are commonly used in Amazonian shamanism. Healers who specialize in perfume medicine are known as "perfumeros." Perfumeros can also use their perfumes for special ceremonies ("ceremonias de perfume") where participants hold a cup of perfume up to their nose and keep inhaling its contents during the entire ceremony, which can last up to an hour. Perfumes in the Amazon are made by steeping flowers and other plants in agua ardiente, sugar cane alcohol. The prolonged inhalation of these perfumes induces a state of inebriation similar to alcohol drunkenness but without the side effects. Powerful visions and insights are often received during such ceremonies.

Another use of flowers, perfumes, and aromatic herbs, is flower baths (*baños de florecimiento*), which are sometimes performed before an Ayahuasca ceremony to prepare the participants by cleansing them.

Encantos

"Encantos" are healing stones and crystals used in Peruvian shamanism for healing. Stones are particularly difficult to find in most of the Amazon jungle, and are therefore particularly treasured. Healing stones are sometimes found in Nature under particular conditions that make them special and magical, or have features resembling those of a power animal or other entities, and sometimes they are simply given or bought. Either way, their healing abilities are recognized and nurtured by the healer who uses them.

These stones are used by laying them on the parts of the body that need healing, and are believed to be capable of extracting heavy energies and illnesses, and restore the normal activities of the parts affected.

As we can see an Ayahuasca ceremony is a ritual specifically designed and refined over millennia to enhance the power of this medicine and facilitate the experience of those who drink it. Despite the absence of light and motion, it is a dynamic event that makes full and intelligent use of sound, music, rhythm, smell, and some other shamanic tools for healing.

Attending an Ayahuasca ceremony brings us back to the ways practiced all over the world since the dawn of humanity for celebration, prayer, and healing. It also teaches modern man a different way of using mind-altering substances: in today's world these substances are very popular, but there is a dire need for new ways and rituals where they can be used with safety and to act positively on those who ingest them.

Ayahuasca ceremonies are a valid model that can inspire us towards new ways of approaching and using all sorts of mind-altering substances. The general desacralization of our world has also affected the way we use these powerful substances – once again native cultures act as powerful reminders of ancient ways that are far from primitive or obsolete, but are part of our human heritage.

The key elements here are not only the attention towards the creation and maintenance of a sacred space, but also the preparatory work, particularly in setting clear intentions for the ritual and each participant.

One last important thing to be aware of when attending a ceremony is the fact that this work affects not only us personally and individually but, through the changes within ourselves, it affects also our families and friends, our communities, the planet we live on, and the whole of Creation. The entire collectivity and the whole planet benefit from the work we do in consciousness as individuals.

THE PERSONAL
EXPERIENCE

A s the deeper contract we have with the medicine is frequently a mysterious one, and as we are often rather unaware of what lies within our souls, the effects of Ayahuasca are sometimes unpredictable and beyond our control. This chapter focuses on the most challenging aspects of this work: the intention is to offer some clear information and guidance that can be helpful when approaching this medicine. This information is not meant to scare anyone, on the contrary, it is meant to help deal with our irrational fears, and provide effective tools should those fears arise in the middle of a ceremony.

First of all it is important to know and remember that, under the guidance of a medicine person with integrity, no one without any serious medical problems and with the proper preparation has ever died from drinking Ayahuasca. When the precautions and preparations illustrated all along in this book are followed, there are absolutely no risks in taking this medicine. Besides users of antidepressants and other medications that affect brain chemistry, who should discontinue these medications at least three months before drinking Ayahuasca, also people who have had important internal surgery should wait at least three to six months as well, depending on the nature of such surgeries and the time needed to recover from them.

People new to this medicine often experience some kind of dying experience: the breathing becomes shallow, it is impossible to move, intense pain is felt in the physical body, the visions can be overwhelmingly strong and fast. All these reactions and the lack of experience often lead some participants to thinking and believing that they are dying. The thought "I am dying" becomes larger and larger, until it is believed with certainty. As a reaction many people begin to feel fear and panic. But, however strong this belief may be, however strong the effects of the medicine, no one dies from it: no one ever has and you will not be the first. Despite the subjective certainty of one's impeding death, this is simply not one of the things this medicine does or can do.

Another concern people have when entering strong mind-altered states is the fear of remaining in these states for the rest of their lives. This stems in particular from tales of people who have used excessive amounts of LSD without being actually prepared and ready for it. Stories of a few such cases have been used and blown out of proportion by governments and the media to warn people against the dangers of hallucinogens and create a collective phobia regarding altered states of consciousness. But no matter how strongly one is affected by the medicine, these effects will eventually taper down within a few hours, and the normal state of consciousness will be regained automatically.

There have been some cases of people whose psyche has been affected in unwelcome ways, sometimes through temporary psychotic breakdowns as I witnessed in the case of a young man in the jungle, who was unexpectedly forced to face the horrors of his time in the army but in the end, if the therapeutic work is well handled, such breakdowns become the cornerstones of a new healthy individual.

It cannot be stressed enough that this work is not for everyone and that we should use the uttermost care when engaging in it. People with serious personality disorders ought to wait until they are solidly grounded before they use any mind-altering substances. I have found the work with consciousness to be the most delicate of endeavors: we need to exercise great patience and care when exploring our own inner landscapes.

Usually it is at the beginning of the ceremony that one feels the strongest effects and is most impacted by the radical changes in consciousness, awareness, and physical state. The reaction is often fear, and when unchecked, that fear can turn into panic. Fear is how the ego expresses its uneasiness with the situation, and how it reacts when it perceives something that it interprets as dangerous to its own survival. Fear is the clearest sign of resistance on the part of the ego regarding any given situation that threatens it. Fear is a very helpful emotion when experienced consciously: it helps us to survive and avoid possibly lethal dangers. Unfortunately many people carry so many fears that these fears, instead of supporting them, prevent them from living altogether. There are healthy fears, and there are irrational fears that become obstacles to one's daily life. There are fears deeply rooted in our psyche through millennia of evolution, and there are fears that stem from education, culture, and personal experiences either in this or other lifetimes. In either case, fear has often the deleterious effect of freezing the flow of our experience to the point of making us incapable of reacting positively to the situation at hand.

In the case of an Ayahuasca ceremony, reacting with excessive fear and panic only worsens the situation, and risks ending up in a "bad trip," an experience where the individual is stuck in an unpleasant situation without any solution in sight. As the main cause of this situation is the unwillingness to experience what is happening, the best way of dealing with it is by reaffirming our willingness to be present and part of the process, even despite our fear. In such cases, simply tell yourself, the medicine, and whatever spiritual guide you may invoke when in need: "I am willing." Simply stating our willingness to stay present helps us to shift out of the fear and back into the flow of the experience. This very simple but powerful mantra has helped countless people who have worked with me over the years, not just during ceremonies but in life in general.

The general attitude is not to try to fight the effects of the medicine, particularly if the experience becomes very unusual or frightening. Facing fear is a recurrent theme during Ayahuasca ceremonies in particular, and spiritual evolution in general. Westerners have become increasingly afraid of fear, and reluctant to look at it. Everywhere we go we need to be able to master any given situation and control our emotions, particularly the emotion of fear. As a culture we have become totally phobic regarding those situations that cause us the most anxiety, in particular dying. The "Vine of Death" becomes then a wonderful tool and guide to help us unravel the sources of our anxieties and fears.

Fear and concern can be triggered by difficulty in breathing or an inability to move, but there is no need to worry because the medicine doesn't provoke respiratory failures or paralysis. Breathing consciously is always a powerful way of relaxing and allowing the experience to flow with ease. After singing, the activity that takes most of my time during ceremonies is reminding people to breathe: to inhale as deeply and gently as possible, and to let go as much as possible upon each exhalation. I find it particularly useful for most to exhale through their mouth: this allows the jaw muscles to relax and induces a deeper state of surrender.

Gentle concentration on the breath allows us to regain a certain feeling of safety and increased awareness. When I lead a ceremony I am particularly aware of how deeply the rich and conscious breathing involved in singing icaros helps me expand my awareness and consciousness, and how easily I can change the quality of my experience through breath and song alone. The trance, altered, and expanded states of consciousness induced by the sole use of singing are common in rituals all over the world, and the breathing involved in singing is one of the main factors in the power of singing.

It feels important here to stress that breath or body postures shouldn't be used to try and control the situation but simply to facilitate the surrendering to it. People with a meditation practice may want to try and avoid their meditation posture and attitude, which sometimes can become an unconscious way of armoring oneself against unpleasant feelings. I have witnessed various cases of experienced meditators, who hold a very Zen and tranquil attitude during the ceremonies and then end up spending the rest of the night throwing up and in a general state of discomfort. This is because during the ceremony they skillfully avoided whatever the medicine needed to do, and once the ceremony was over and they relaxed their physical and mental postures, the medicine started doing its work, often without the support of the ceremonial space, which had long been closed.

I usually advise people who are stuck in their usual thought patterns to put their hands on their bellies and breathe deeply, feeling their hands rise and fall with their breath. If familiar thoughts (those famous "old records") persist, one can ask oneself what he or she is afraid of experiencing and feeling: the mind is usually the best refuge one can find to run away from fully experiencing something. Thinking about something rather than directly experiencing it gives us often just enough distance: it is a common survival strategy designed to help us feel less, but also one that prevents us from being fully present. We remove ourselves from the experience at hand and seek refuge in the tiny tower of our mind. From that little place we look out onto the world, scouting for dangers, devising strategies and courses of action, and try to make sense of an existence by which we often feel overwhelmed.

Breathing helps us shift very quickly and effectively from our little minds to a less rigid and more expanded feeling state. From this place, which is essentially the judgment-free space of the heart, we can finally embrace all sorts of resisted experiences and allow ourselves to have whatever emotional reaction without self-censorship.

A common concern for people new to this kind of healing practice comes from old and still enforced governmental propaganda about the use of psyche-delics – starting in the 1960's many stories have been circulated about people taking LSD and losing their minds forever. Even though a minority of these reports may have been true, they were often taken out of context and exaggerated. The question is: In the case of a radical departure from my habitual state of consciousness under the effects of Ayahuasca, will I be able to return to my normal state? The answer is: Yes. No matter how strong the experience may be, the effects of Ayahuasca are temporary. I usually say jokingly to people with such concerns that they don't pay me nearly enough to keep them altered for the rest of their lives. But honestly, I have so far never seen anybody actually lose their mind, but have witnessed the healing of many.

The question inevitably resurfaces when one is feeling overwhelmed by intense bodily sensations and visions: sometimes the visions are so strong and fast that the mind is totally unable to process them as usual, and the individual experiencing them wonders whether he or she is going mad. But such is not the case: eventually the flow of the visions slows down and stops.

Being able to comprehend and process such occasionally vast amounts of information is tantalizing – once again it is best to go with the flow rather than try to control the experience: sometimes the meaning and nature of certain visions isn't revealed until much later after the ceremony. And even when certain visions occur so rapidly that we can't hold on to them, it is beneficial to trust that the experience, even when beyond our understanding, has happened and resides somewhere in our being. This was the case for me during my apprenticeship: I was dieting the Datura plant and when the time came for me to drink an Ayahuasca brew that contained Datura flowers, I would end up spending most of the ceremonies in a sort of sleep, from which I would be awakened only at the end of the ceremony. The experience was confusing and irritating at first as I saw no benefit in participating in a ceremony, of which I could remember nothing at all. However, I soon realized that the quality of my daily meditation had acquired a crystalline quality until then unknown to me, and eventually I stopped trying to make sense of the whole process and let go of my need to rationally grasp all of it.

What is most frightening to us is also what on some deep level we crave the most: the lessening of the ego's grip on our existence. This release is the stuff of spiritual legends, something we look for and yet run away from at the same time. The temporary but sometimes sudden eclipse of the rational mind can be a daunting experience: when the sense of separation created by the mind diminishes, we can be often catapulted into an experience of total oneness with everything within and without time and space. This can be sometimes a truly overwhelming one for some people. Without a doubt, to know and experience Infinity and Eternity first hand can be disorienting or scary to the ego.

In such states of expansion one can easily access all sorts of beliefs and experiences stored in the collective and universal consciousness, from material to organic and spiritual realities, both heard and unheard of. What is normally and essentially a selective perception of the Universe (as well as our deeply personal interpretation of it) can become an oceanic experience with no shore in sight. The experience of such unity and intrinsic connection and communication across all of Creation is also one the deepest healing experiences that entheogens such as Ayahuasca offer to us.

The sudden connection to the collective unconscious puts us sometimes in the position of having to integrate all sorts of past suffering and abuse that need healing. Some people experience past events that are not necessarily personal, even though they may mirror some individual issues and wounds, but that are simply part of the collectivity such as wars and violent conflicts of all kinds. An example of this was the experience of a woman who during a ceremony relived an instance of Native Americans pillaging a settlement of pioneers and raping many women, among which was this very woman. She was completely shocked by what she saw and felt so for many hours afterwards until she was made aware that this hadn't been necessarily something she had experienced personally in a previous life, but that at the same time it may have reflected something that resonated with her own personal issues as a woman, or that simply it was something hanging in the collective consciousness that she had somehow agreed to integrate.

On other occasions, the often intensely earthy energy of this particular medicine makes us aware of our intrinsic communion with everything and everyone on this planet, thus freeing us from the alienation we so often suffer from since the advent of the modern scientific frame of mind.

Loss of control of the physical body can also be a source of concern, particularly in regards to the inability to move or to control one's bowel movements. Drinking Ayahuasca is rarely a clean and proper activity: there is a lot of cleansing going on - often vomiting, retching, spitting, and defecating are involved as part of the process. One is not expected to remain totally in control, and there is no reason to feel any shame regarding these bodily functions, which are totally natural.

A lot of people are very reluctant to engage in any activity that will almost certainly involve vomiting, which they associate with very unpleasant past experiences, such as illnesses, episodes of food poisoning, or excessive alcohol consumption, either personal or by close relations. Vomiting can occur repeatedly until the effects of the medicine taper off and sometimes a few hours after the ceremony is over. Vomiting is not a way of the body of expelling some kind of poison present in the medicine itself, but one of the healing effects of the medicine, which is per se not toxic.

Often vomiting is preceded by nausea and stomach cramps: signs that the medicine is working its way through our system and cleansing it. Sometimes the vomiting can be rather prolonged and extenuating: this is not a particularly pleasant experience, but definitely a positive one as it indicates a deep and long-overdue cleansing. Sometimes the vomiting proper is preceded by long periods of dry heaving: the person tries to expel something but nothing comes out. In these cases it is helpful to remind oneself that the rhythm of the medicine isn't necessarily the same as the one of our minds, and that whatever needs to come out of the body will do so in its own time.

Reluctance to let go can manifest as a difficulty to let go on a physical level as well. For many, myself included, the experience with Ayahuasca changes radically after vomiting. Some people cannot move into the next phase of their experience until they physically throw up: in such cases, facilitating through songs or other means the onset of vomiting can open doors that have remained until then closed. Once the fear of vomiting has been overcome through the act of vomiting itself, we can continue our journey with more ease. What ends up coming out of the physical body are the materialized aspects of old patterns, emotions, and traumas that have been in our consciousness for such a long time that they have taken on a physical form, often causing the body to become ill.

A friend of mine was able over the course of two very intense ceremonies to let go, both through vomiting and defecating, of the pain she had held inside herself for many years as a result of a very important but abusive love relationship. For months prior to these ceremonies she had had major digestive issues, which eased and ended soon afterwards as a result of this healing.

In the long run it is these thoughts and feelings that become toxic, and it is these poisons that the medicine expels on all levels of our being, including the physical. In shamanism, all diseases are first and foremost a manifestation of an illness of the soul and spirit, therefore healing happens both on the physical and non-physical levels simultaneously. And so it happens that one can have the distinct experience that what one is expelling isn't simply bile or feces, but old dynamics, patterns, and emotions that were once useful but have since become noxious.

As I have mentioned earlier, the cleansing process is often accompanied by visions of these heavy energies, sometimes leaving the body, sometimes covering it. These visions can be of dark snakes, insects, and scary creatures. Those "monsters" are not out there to get us, but are simply manifestations of the heavy energies we hold within: as the medicine makes us aware of them, it makes them also visible to our inner eye. The sight of these heavy energies can be at times terrifying, but they remain totally harmless: they are being shown for us to become aware of what we carry inside and what the medicine is helping us release. The best attitude is not to react against these visions but, if anything, try to understand where they come from and what lessons they may have for us that we have until now failed to learn.

It happened once during a ceremony that I asked a participant whether she was receiving what she had come looking for. The answer she gave me was negative: she had come to experience some inner light but was nevertheless constantly surrounded by dark energies that no matter how hard she tried to push away, wouldn't leave her alone. After being advised to stop rejecting these energies but rather welcome them, she started sobbing and cried on and off for the rest of the ceremony. She was being apologetic about it but it was clear that she was finally receiving the healing that she needed, and was eventually very grateful for the experience.

Sometimes the visions indicate down to the cellular and DNA level the exact location of certain diseases or imbalances, sometimes it is on a soul level that the disorder is shown and worked on. It is important to be aware that the ingestion of Ayahuasca doesn't necessarily imply the legendary visions that have made this medicine popular in our times. My teacher, Don Francisco Montes, believes that when people don't experience any visions it's because they are receiving healing, and vice versa. The visionary aspect of this medicine is not the essential part of this work – some people are highly visual, some aren't. Lack of visions doesn't mean the medicine isn't working, it's just that it isn't affecting the individual on the visual plane. The essence of this work isn't otherworldly colorful visions but healing.

For some people the initial experience with Ayahuasca is simply a cleansing that is felt on the physical plane and nothing else – this may be a particularly difficult process for those who start working with this medicine in their later years and have held on to certain noxious energies for many many years. It is only when the most physical layers are cleansed that the medicine can start affecting the psyche with insights and sometimes visions. To those truly interested in an in-depth work with this medicine, I almost always recommend an initial series of at least three ceremonies so that they can benefit from this medicine on all levels.

Discouragement and frustration are not uncommon, but perseverance is highly rewarding in all cases I have encountered. It is not at all uncommon for people drinking this medicine for the first time to be so turned off by the overall unpleasantness of their experience that they swear never to drink it again. In those cases I always ask them to take some time for the experience to be fully integrated before shutting the door closed forever on this wonderful medicine.

Perhaps the most frustrating result of ingesting Ayahuasca is when nothing at all seems to happen and the person leaves the ceremony feeling empty-handed and disappointed. This may be due to a physiological situation where the body isn't capable of assimilating the medicine properly, like for people with a clinical history of depression, or with metabolic difficulties. On most other instances this is due to unconscious resistances to the medicine and its effects, an inability to surrender, the resurfacing of old patterns that prevent one from letting go, or a negative attitude towards the experience or the medicine. In such cases it is really up to the individual whether they are willing and ready to address these issues, and whether the environment and the guide are supportive enough to overcome these limitations. Dealing with resistances, questioning their validity instead of buying into them, is very rewarding. In the absence of resistance all experience flows naturally and easily from onset until completion. As a medicine person my goal is to free from any obstacles the path of the medicine so she can do her work in as easy a way as possible.

Some people think that the use of Ayahuasca implies some kind of belief system or spiritual path they need to adhere to in order for it to "work." As far as I am concerned this belief is erroneous: Ayahuasca is simply a medicine and a tool, not a religion, and can be used by anybody as long as they don't believe its use goes against their current belief system. Openness of heart and mind, and a respectful and humble attitude are all that is required.

Over the years I have encountered quite a few people who are convinced that "Ayahuasca is not their medicine." They have drunk a few times and now they claim that, "it just wasn't for them," or there was no connection. Even though I'll concede that drinking Ayahuasca is not for everybody, I can always tell when the person in front of me has hit along the road a major resistance that was not dealt with, or that the person was not yet quite ready to deal with. We rationalize and create stories to explain an event or other, and in so doing we often create perfect excuses for our decisions and actions. Allowing ourselves to question our motives and probing our lives with honesty often reveal fears and insecurities that for most are best left unexamined. Personally I have found the path of awareness to be more fulfilling than denial and strive to bring more and more clarity into my life whenever possible. There have been times when I have recoiled in shame once I was finally willing to look into the face of the naked truth: the stories I had created and told myself and others to protect myself from feeling hurt, confused, or scared! That the time to let go of our defenses hasn't quite arrived yet is of little importance as time is of little relevance: eventually we will all lower our masks as the Gates of Heaven can be crossed only when we let go of our personalities and let our divine essence shine.

In the light of all this, it is of paramount importance that the people drinking Ayahuasca for the first time or with a new guide share their medical history and all the concerns they may feel well before a ceremony. If for whatever reason they don't feel comfortable doing so, then it is best not to drink altogether, at least for the time being. Working with Ayahuasca entails a great deal of trust in oneself and all the people involved in the ceremony: if such trust is lacking, it is better to wait for another occasion.

THE PSYCHIC MIRROR OF CEREMONIAL SPACE

It is not unusual for people to complain during or after the ceremony about the guide, the setting, or more often about other people in attendance. Under the influence of Ayahuasca one is not immune to project undesired aspects of oneself onto others or the environment – actually, those projections are often larger than life: people get upset and very judgmental of others. This is a classic blessing in disguise as others are so generously willing to host our projections so that we can see through them and gain deeper awareness of our patterns, and eventually release them.

An Ayahuasca ceremony is like an enhanced version of daily life, and in it some familiar and some secret aspects of ourselves make their appearance. It is a good thing to remind oneself of certain pitfalls one may have a tendency to create over and over again, such as giving one's power away to some authority figure, e.g., the shaman, or certain negative judgments about people or situations. As with all other emotions coming up during a ceremony, simply sit back and watch yourself and your ways of being: are these recurrent themes in your life? Are you happy simply reacting to them in your usual way or would you rather take advantage of the situation and look at them more closely, and perhaps find the reasons for such behaviors? There are no coincidences, and often we find ourselves sitting in ceremony with exactly the kind of people needed to heal certain aspects of ourselves, no matter how annoying their presence may seem at first.

This reminds me of a story a friend related to me about a ceremony where someone had been screaming for a very long time. After a while someone angrily reacted by saying out loud, "Shut up! You are ruining my experience!," to which my friend wisely responded, "He IS your experience."

Assuming total responsibility for yourself, your choices, and experiences is the sign of true maturity. Blaming everything and everybody else only keeps us in a place of powerlessness and unconsciousness. So when you start getting all upset at somebody, be grateful and remember that a new powerful lesson and chance for healing has just begun! Of course we never react with enthusiasm in such cases. On the contrary, we start resenting people for mirroring back to us aspects of ourselves that we don't like and have invested much energy in avoiding.

As we are with ourselves, so are we with others: we judge, chastise, ridicule, reprimand, and generally reject others because their behavior reminds us of parts of ourselves we'd rather not look at. It happens all the time, including among people who have gathered to drink Ayahuasca: insecurities, fears, judgments, envies and jealousies, group dynamics, power plays – all the dramas of our personal lives can be acted out with any group of people.

Because of the temporary altered state of consciousness induced by Ayahuasca, people often say after a ceremony that "they're going back to their lives," when there is never such a separation and indeed the picture we gather of all the thoughts and emotions we experience during a ceremony is actually a far more complete and accurate than the edited version of ourselves we are constantly trying to sell to others or ourselves.

Eventually the ceremonial space turns into a hall of mirrors where cherished and resisted parts of ourselves make their appearance. Once in the jungle I left soon after the closing of a ceremony with a friend who seemed rather annoyed with the prolonged humming of another participant. It was clear to me that leaving the space was the easiest solution available and we gently made our way back to our huts while of course discussing proper and improper ceremonial etiquette. My friend pointed out the need in his opinion for a common set of rules that, when observed by all at all times, would not only benefit each participant but the flow of the ceremony as well. Misbehavior then, I gathered, would not only be offending to others but also to the ceremony itself. I pointed out to my friend that seemingly he had been the only one bothered by this other person's humming and that therefore it wasn't exactly a public case but a very personal one. I also reminded my friend that one of his main intentions for being in the jungle was to let go of self-judgment and the insecurity that results from non-acceptance. We talked about the ways we project onto others our own self-criticism and in the end what could have been another pointless rant about the lack of respect and education of others became a precious opportunity to explore the theme of inadequacy.

Ayahuasca ceremonies are fairly simple rituals. My friend and teacher Joseph Kramer explained to me years ago that a ritual is basically something "with a beginning, an end, and something in the middle." For me that "something in the middle" ought to be as empty and uncluttered as possible in order to give a blank slate upon which each participant can project his own personal stuff and supportive of one's becoming aware of one's own projections. Ayahuasca ceremonies are not performances but occasions where our hurt selves can come out without fear of judgment or rejection. In my work I ask each participant to hold their space, i.e., not worry about what goes on around them during the ceremony, but also remind them that we are among sisters and brothers and they should not feel self-conscious but just let themselves be exactly as they need to be.

Most recently I had a young woman in a ceremony who clearly needed to scream. A lot. So, for three consecutive ceremonies she spent the entire time in my living room making all the noise she needed to make while we were in the temple next door.

It's nice to be in a safe space where we feel there is a place and time for everybody to be whoever they need to be, no matter how outlandish or noisy. In the end I have learnt that with an open mind, some common sense, and patience, there is space for everybody and everyone's stories. For me it's a blessing to host and witness the ever-changing groups of people who come and work with me, in mutual support, respect, and laughter.

Spirit Guides

Usually at the beginning and during an Ayahuasca ceremony a safe and sacred space is created to ward off potentially negative energies, and all sorts of healing energies and guides are invoked. Power animals, the spirit of the medicine or of other plant teachers, angels and spiritual guides as well as doctor spirits are among those energies that frequently visit us. It is important to remember that when healing is sincerely sought, the whole Universe supports us in our task. Some of these energies may be familiar while others may be totally foreign and even alien, some are connected to past worlds and civilizations, and some to realities beyond time.

However, it sometimes happens that all sorts of discarnate energies from the astral realm may appear during a ceremony as well. If you are not sure whether those visiting energies are there to support you in your process, simply ask them, "Are you here to help me?" You will get a clear and truthful answer, and if they are not there to help you, thank them for their visit and kindly ask them to leave as you are presently busy. If they are indeed just passing energies, as opposed to aspects of your own self, they will leave. This is a good way of keeping the ceremonial space free from unnecessary astral energies and therefore being able to conduct your work without distractions.

An example of this came from someone who kept encountering in his visions many characters one after another. He kept asking whether they were there to help him and, after receiving a negative answer, he would gently send them away until an energy that appeared to him in the form of his long-deceased younger sister came to him to guide him for the rest of the ceremony and eventually took him to a very special place where some divine entity shared with him much wisdom and knowledge.

THE VISIONS

Ayahuasca, like other entheogens and psychedelic substances, has the ability to provoke all sorts of visions. Some of these are particular to the person drinking it, often stemming from one's own personal background; others are surprisingly alien and exotic, or are characteristic of the medicine itself, such as visions of snakes, jaguars, and other animals and energies particular of the Amazon region from where this medicine comes. People can experience in vivid images the resurgence of familiar figures and symbols deeply seated in one's consciousness, such as those coming from one's religious beliefs and culture. For some it will be Christian, Jewish, or Buddhist imagery, for others it will be representations of the Universe or the physical body as one believes them to be, such as those informed by the belief in a system of chakras, or other views of the physical world varying from mythological to quantum physics and beyond.

Quite often our view of ourselves and the Cosmos are radically deepened during the Ayahuasca journey:

a phenomenon that is likely to transform individuals in their beliefs, not only at the level of the mind, but more profoundly, at the level of the soul. Seeing is believing, and even though such visions are clearly catalyzed by the medicine, they are perceived and experienced as true. The effect of expanding beyond one's beliefs is profound – the stretching of our view of the world and ourselves affects our psyches and allows for a reordering of personal priorities and values. Under the right conditions such visions are not confusing, but on the contrary, they let us make better sense of the world inside and outside ourselves. Sometimes people visit realms they didn't know existed, other times people are able to connect with ancient or extraterrestrial civilizations, at other it is a connection with angelical beings and divine energies. The experience of meeting and interacting with God or other transcendental entities is not uncommon. Ayahuasca is an entheogen, i.e., a substance capable of catalyzing an experience of the Divine. It is known as a sacred medicine because it opens the way to the sacred and the transcendental - dimensions often eluding modern man but that we are all to a certain degree attracted to.

The repercussions of ecstatic visions on the individual are always profound. In light of such experience, and from such an expanded point of view, our perception and understanding of who we are changes radically, as does our perception of the world around us. The experiential reconnection with what we intuitively feel is the very core of our nature, i.e., the spiritual center that is our true identity beyond all physical forms and mental or psychological constructs, has been regarded by those mystics who throughout the ages have had such experiences as the most fulfilling of all.

Such transcendental religious or mystical experiences are often the result of many years of meditation or other spiritual practices, but can occur spontaneously to those who are karmically ready for it, or through "fortuitous" events or Divine Grace. In reality all spiritual epiphanies are equally valid, no matter how they manifested. Spiritual disciplines are only tools to achieve such states of consciousness and in many cases they are even unnecessary.

However, the experience of the Divine in all its power and glory is not something to be taken lightly – in various spiritual traditions the direct encounter with God is deemed dangerous and only safely available to those of pure heart and mind. The reason for this way of thinking is that the closer one gets to God, the higher the vibratory field, and sometimes people are simply not prepared for such an energetic leap in consciousness. Some people lose their connection with reality (and there is a good reason to believe that many such individuals are presently spending their days in psychiatric institutions), some others simply blank out the whole experience. In both cases the individual is overwhelmed by the experience and unable to integrate it harmoniously – the fact that these experiences are often beyond the power of words to describe only make the task more difficult. The radically transformative power of the mystical experience under the influence of entheogens demands great presence from those who undergo it. The fact that such leaps in consciousness can happen so quickly requires total surrender and openness of mind and spirit.

In many circles the use of entheogens is regarded as some sort of shortcut on the spiritual path; what is not taken into account by this assessment is the fact that the integration of such experiences is often long and demanding on the part of the spiritual seeker. Everybody is touched by Ayahuasca, but permanent changes are less obvious to manifest. In most cases though such encounters are highly positive and spark a renewed interest in spirituality and a desire to live a life more in accordance with one's heart, often leading the individual beyond selfish concerns and more towards socially aware and compassionate choices.

My final decision to become an ayahuasquero was taken while under the effects of Ayahuasca. What was unusual was not the choice to study and practice plant medicine: the amazing thing was that for the first time in my life I was taking a decision where none of my usual ego-centered concerns were taken into consideration. Deciding to be of service to this medicine rather than pursuing my own goals was revolutionary for me, even more so was the discovery a year after this decision that, as a result of this selfless decision, I was receiving from the Universe more than I had ever received or thought possible before while I was busy pursuing my own egoic goals.

The mystical experience is erroneously perceived as an extraordinary state of grace, or even worse as the "ultimate high," only available to a fortunate few. In reality such events are the birthright of all human beings as creatures who are integral part and not dissociated from the Divine. The main religions of this world are lead by a priestly caste that has often monopolized all access to God, and have popularized the belief that we are somehow incapable or unworthy of true divine union. The shamanistic view, as well as that of non-hierarchical spiritual disciplines, differs from this viewpoint and doesn't look with suspicion upon all those who undergo a deeply spiritual experience – on the contrary, it is encouraged, honored and viewed with respect.

To regard traditional spiritual belief systems such as those of the people of the Amazon basin as animistic is highly reductive: in fact these cultures fully acknowledge the presence of the Divine in everything and everybody without distinction. As God is not a separate entity from Its creations, everything is imbued with Its energy and everybody is naturally endowed with the ability to become fully conscious of their own divine essence and recognize it in everything. The immanent presence of God is celebrated, and the territories of the invisible are explored as integral part of the human experience. The shamanic experience is one of unmediated, direct contact with the Divine, and therein lies its power.

The validity of extraordinary visions depends on the willingness of the individual to accept their experience as real, and not just the product of intoxication. Hallucinations, by definition, are those things we see but which do not exist. On the other hand, visions are the result of being better able to see reality in deeper detail. Often being able to differentiate between hallucinations and visions is a difficult task, but one shouldn't worry too much about it: one's gut feelings are the best judge in realizing what is indeed valid and meaningful. What is important is to decipher sooner or later the real meaning of certain visions. Some visions are quite literal while others are more symbolic. In the case of many visions, it is wise to understand why we are having such visions rather than taking them at face value. Is the vision of a family member's death a real occurrence or the resurfacing of old fears or other? Perhaps such vision is only meant to reawaken certain dynamics that need healing, and perhaps it is a premonition of future events. The main problem is that what can be perceived as happening in the present moment during a ceremony is actually happening in a psychic space out of time and space, so it is very difficult to ascertain the validity of certain details, and their true meaning can sometimes be assessed only after some time.

Beside the appearance of archetypes from the collective unconscious, often people have visions that are not specifically personal but belong to the collective at large. The individual becomes a mirror of the Macrocosm, and global issues such as the ecology, war, or the Feminine, make their appearance in our consciousness for us to deal with and integrate. The work done individually is actually instrumental in the collective solution of such conflicts: a single person may not be able to change the world but they can definitely help make it a better place by integrating certain limiting beliefs and viewpoints that prevent us from applying new and innovative solutions to old problems.

The validity of particularly traumatic experiences and of suppressed memories that may come to one's awareness under the effects of Ayahuasca or other altered states of consciousness, have always been a question of debate since the beginning of hypnotherapy and psychoanalysis and continue to be examined by most contemporary healing modalities. Among these, the most delicate ones are what people call "past life memories" and memories of childhood sexual abuse. It is difficult, if not impossible, to assess with certainty the validity of these memories. For me the best approach is to ask oneself how these memories resonate with oneself. Whether these memories are literal or symbolic is not really the main issue: we would better ask ourselves what these images are meant to reveal and teach to us at this time.

If the resurfacing of such memories is accompanied with a strong reaction, then one can safely assume that the themes they present are ripe for examination and healing, whether they relate to actual events or not. It is my belief that whatever may be left over and subsequently resurfaces from past lives are aspects of ourselves that haven't yet been integrated. In the present moment we hold all past, present, and future, and usually what is still present in our consciousness from past experiences, whether from this or other past lives, is here for us to examine and learn from, so that it can be let go of.

It is always wise to take these visions and "memories" not too personally and yet acknowledge their relevance as part of our experience rather than exercise further denial or simple dismissal. Last but not least, it is important to remind oneself that whatever vision of the future one may encounter, this vision is only one among infinite possibilities and not something that will necessarily manifest exactly as we saw it during a ceremony.

During a ceremony it is not uncommon to be visited not only by friends and family, long dead or still alive, but also by entities of various nature that appear in order to help heal the individual. Sometimes it is a familiar energy, like that of a guardian angel or power animal, while at other times they are seen for the very first time, like spirit doctors or plant spirits.

Once again, if you are visited by an energy that you are not sure 100% to be there to support you in your healing, simply ask it, "Are you here to help me?" You will get a clear answer and if they are not there to help you, ask them kindly to leave you and they will leave. It is better to leave curious discarnate energies out of the ceremonial space rather than allow an astral circus to pitch its tent inside of it.

Furthermore there are a few recurring kinds of images that appear over and over again during Ayahuasca ceremonies; these are the symbolic and living elements of Peruvian spirituality and cosmology, and they are the Snake, the Jaguar and the Puma, and the Condor and the Eagle.

The Snake

The spirit of Ayahuasca is famous for appearing in the shape of a snake, brilliantly colored or translucent with light. The snake is a universal symbol of medicine, and in Peru this animal is not only the symbol of healing but also of wisdom.

The snake is the king of the Underworld, and holds the powers of the Earth. The cosmic serpents Sachamama and Yakumama are the bringers of rain, life, and fertility, and have been revered in Peru for millennia. It is believed that deep in the jungle, in the most inaccessible and swampy areas, lives Sachamama (the Mother of the Forest), a giant snake several meters in diameter and some tens of meters long. Due to its large size it leads a sedentary life with movements that are almost imperceptible to the human eye and the animals that are thus unable to notice it. With the passing of time its body resembles an old fallen tree with mosses, lichens, shrubs, and lianas growing over it. Every seventy years this snake is believed to go down the rivers to the sea, home to the other snake, the Yacumama or Mother of the Waters, and spawns there before returning home. This cycle has been repeated and renewed since time immemorial.

According to Inca legend, the Sachamama is an ancient deity in charge with its twin sister Yacumama to unite the three worlds called Hanan Pacha or Upper World, Kay Pacha or Middle World, and Uku Pacha or Underworld.

It is no strange coincidence that the energy of a medicine like Ayahuasca, capable of providing healing and guidance, appears to people from all over the world in the shape of a large snake, a snake that sometimes devours us to be reborn anew from its entrails, and sometimes talks to us with great wisdom and acuity. The healing power of Ayahuasca is the very energy of the Earth, coupled with the divine intelligence symbolized by the Sun that gives her light and nourishment, and propels her towards the Heavens. The way the Ayahuasca vine grows in the jungle has reminded Westerner researchers of a DNA strand: a perfect helix wrapping her trunk around a tree.[10] The fact that this vine looks just like a snake climbing a tree only adds to the idea of a plant richly connected with the symbolism and power of snakes.

---

10   This idea has been explored by the author Jeremy Narby in the book *The Cosmic Serpent*, Penguin/Putnam, 1998.

Because of its connection to the Earth, the spirit of Ayahuasca is often perceived as feminine, and many refer to this energy as "Mother Ayahuasca" or "Grandmother Ayahuasca." Some shamans on the other hand see this vine as more masculine, as opposed to the Chakruna plant, which is seen as more feminine. In the end all that can be noted is that its various manifestations clearly transcend gender or other labels.

The Jaguar and the Puma

Jaguars and pumas are the most powerful animals walking this part of Earth, whether in the jungle or the mountains. Their power is feared and respected. They are a symbol of the power of manifestation on this plane of reality, and not surprisingly did the ancient Incas build their capital city of Cuzco, which in the Quechua language means "navel," in the shape of a puma.

The vision of a jaguar during a ceremony can be greatly auspicious, provided one doesn't fall prey to fear: the power to create and rule justly can only be in the hands of the fearless and courageous.

Shamans often shape-shift into jaguars when they need their power to either attack or protect themselves from enemies.

The archetypal energy and power of the jaguar and the puma can be invoked for all sorts of human activities. Soon after the purchase of my land in Pisac needed to conduct my work with Ayahuasca, I went on a pilgrimage to the Island of the Sun in Bolivia and spent a whole day meditating by the sacred Puma

Rock there. I invoked the energy of the puma to support me and everyone involved in the creation of my healing center and two days later did the same by the ruin known as the Temple of the Puma in the archeological site of Tiahuanaco. I asked for the courage and strength I needed to make this project a reality and received these gifts aplenty.

The Condor and the Eagle

Condors and eagles are the sovereign animals of the sky. As the creatures closest to the Heavens, they are symbols of spiritual energy and the embodiment of man's highest values. Their acute sense of sight is called upon when one needs clarity. Their connection to the high skies makes the condor and the eagle perfect messengers of the Divine, and symbols of the ability to transcend the earthly realms and limitations. Moreover, flying well above the ground allows us to see certain situations from a more expanded viewpoint and better understand them in their totality. Traditionally these powerful creatures are the perfect vehicles for shamanic flights, either to distant lands or other dimensions.

The condor and the eagle are the subject of an ancient Inca prophecy that says that this is the time when the Eagle of North America and the Condor of South America fly together, which symbolizes the Earth's reawakening and return to balance and harmony.

Anybody visiting Peru will be offered to buy a trinket, either a painting or carving, depicting what is referred to as "the Inca Triad." This is a representation of the three animals and archetypes we have just mentioned: the snake, the puma or jaguar, and the condor. These key animals symbolize the three levels of reality of Peruvian cosmology: Hanan Pacha, Kay Pacha and Uku Pacha. Each animal is also associated with specific qualities: healing and wisdom for the Snake; power, strength and courage for the Puma/Jaguar; love and divine light for the Condor.

One of the teachings connected with this trio of powerful energies calls for the integration of all levels of reality: it says that wisdom, when it fails to be expressed and manifested on the everyday level of reality, isn't worth much at all. It also says that if power and courage aren't illumined with Divine Light and Love it can easily become dangerous. The goal of human endeavors is then a courageous and powerful course of action informed with wisdom and blessed with divine energy.

HEALING WITH AYAHUASCA AND INTEGRATION

A person stands in front of a window at sunset, watching the end of the day until it gets dark outside and eventually all that one sees is one's own reflection in the window. This is what drinking Ayahuasca entails: a shift of attention from the world outside to our inner worlds. It is like watching chapters in the movie of our lives, with deleted or half-forgotten scenes reappearing on the screen of our awareness. Sometimes the movie is all too familiar and a source of discouragement. But the medicine also allows us to look at these scenes from a different point of view and we can seize deeper meanings that had been until then elusive, to the point of clearly understanding why we have invited certain experiences or relationships into our lives. The shift in awareness and the expanded state of consciousness allow the individual to perceive things from a different viewpoint and identity: the "cleansing of the doors of perception" is not just superficial, but affects the psyche and the spirit, so that our understanding is greatly improved by the increased ability to switch viewpoint.

One of the most powerful experiences I have ever had with this medicine happened right after the closing of the first ceremony I attended in the Peruvian Amazon: someone had made a well-intentioned remark about me, but one I didn't like and which upset me as I felt that no-one in the world was really seeing me for who I was. I brooded in my misery and was considering leaving the ceremonial space for a place by the river, where I thought I could scream out all my anger. Unfortunately I was in no shape to go anywhere, which only added to my frustration, so I kept fantasizing about the place and moment in which I could finally release all these feelings. This went on and on until my viewpoint shifted in a totally unexpected way: instead of being stuck in my usual victim mode, I suddenly realized the extent to which I was creating this whole drama for myself, meaning that I had the courage and honesty to admit to myself that I was the sole responsible person for how I was feeling in that moment and that no amount of blaming others or the world was going to get me out of it. The shift from victimhood to accepting responsibility without judgment had me reach for the nearest bucket as I violently purged this old pattern out of my body and soul, and I spent the rest of the night feeling the expansion and freedom of my being without the constraint of this mental and psychic cage of victimization I had been living in for most of my life.

The temporarily lessened grip of the ego allows for a greater capacity to look at ourselves and our lives from an expanded sense of self. Despite our best efforts, it is the very energy of the ego that keeps everything under control and beyond change. The demise of the ego is what really allows us to get in touch with our emotions, our hearts, and our souls.

Under the effects of the medicine there can also occur a shift in the way we perceive our own judgments and mental constructs. With enough detachment, we can stop identifying with them and observe them for what they really are – amazingly curious and interesting creations. The reason the human race has been exploring countless ways of attaining altered states of consciousness, from meditation to trance-inducing rituals, is not because we are trying to escape reality, but to access with our conscious awareness the totality of who we are. We intuit that we are more than the sum of our minds and physical bodies, and have developed through the ages techniques that allow us to reconnect with the most transcendent aspects of our existence. This drive is universal among human beings – some societies cultivate it, others repress it. Philosophers and mystics from India have mapped perhaps better than anyone the dynamics of human consciousness and have developed techniques that are essentially designed to quiet the mind in order to evolve in consciousness. It is their belief that the main obstacle towards personal freedom and happiness is constituted by the ego, which colors everything we experience and clouds it with mistaken perceptions, ideas, and memories that prevent us from accessing the deeper truths of our essence. Ayahuasca, just like meditation but in an often more rapid fashion, allows

163

us to pierce through the levels of ignorance and conditioning (the world of appearances and illusion called Maya), and reconnect with our true spiritual identity.

The movie of our lives that is being shown to us under the influence of Ayahuasca changes radically in meaning as we become better able to see which parts are simply dramas and which are truly essential, which aspects keep us locked in suffering, and which empower us. The way this process unfolds is unique to each individual according to personal history and state. Sometimes the medicine's ways are familiar, and sometimes they offer a radical departure from our way of being and functioning. In either case the medicine seems to be filled with an intelligence capable of taking us from a place of alienation and suffering to one of wholeness: its energy and wisdom lead us right to where we need to go, and guide us through what we need to do in order to heal. This may sound farfetched and suspicious, but it is the experience of most of those who have used this medicine.

The fact that a brew of two different plants seems filled with an undeniably rich energy and intelligence that go beyond what we may attribute to the effects of a psychotropic substance on our brain chemistry is a pretty daunting phenomenon, but one that is validated again and again by people from all cultures and backgrounds. The vibration of this energy is perceived differently by each individual, but it is always experienced as benign, incredibly wise and intelligent, and healing.

Working with Ayahuasca can be a once in a lifetime experience, or one that is repeated whenever the individual feels the need for it. As it's been mentioned before, sometimes the benefits are dramatic and radical, sometimes they are more subtle but equally profound. The path of each soul is not a straight line but one with several twists and detours, peaks and plateaux – only actually walking it gives us a clear image and experience of it.

Often people drink Ayahuasca with the hope and intention of getting a clearer view of their life paths and the choices that best suit their desire to evolve and be happy. Sometimes we receive clear guidance, and sometimes the medicine takes us instead through other inner landscapes that need healing and attention before any life choices are taken. No matter where we are on our paths, we can trust this medicine to help us grow further into wholeness and inner harmony. To achieve all this nothing extraordinary is required, except for a willingness to change and evolve, and trust in the medicine to support us in our process.

Change is often wished for as much as it is feared. Change implies questioning and challenging one's own viewpoints and often allowing them to be replaced by new ways of seeing. This process entails the exercise of sincere and deep forgiveness, which is the only way of substantially shifting out of the blaming paradigm that often paralyzes us in our evolution. If someone is unwilling to let go and forgive oneself and others, then chances of real change become fairly diminished. In my own experience, forgiveness is the sweetest and most powerful of medicines.

Letting go of the old can also involve diving into the unknown: we move away from the familiarity of

165

our daily lives into uncharted territories and explore new ways of being in the world. Such change can be truly challenging at times, but it is often inevitable as we can't expect change without changing ourselves. The letting go of old identities and personal dynamics may throw us into confusion as the mask we have worn disintegrates in front of our eyes. We may wonder who is really the person behind that mask: the loss of identities can be challenging and I invite people who undergo that process to allow themselves to feel confused and to not know rather than scrambling to find some new identity to fill in the void. We look for transcendence, which ultimately entails the loss of the ego, and yet the experience of egolessness can be frightening but if welcomed, it offers the gifts of expansion and direct connection to Source.

The period following the direct work with the medicine is indeed the most important: without proper integration of the experience and the application of its teachings, all the positive results of drinking Ayahuasca can dissolve as quickly as they as they made their appearance.[11]

The Hero's journey does not end with the discovery of the treasure after a long journey through many dangers, but only when the Hero returns home with his treasure. Drinking Ayahuasca is such a journey: it allows us to finally visit a magical place filled with treasures. We leave this place with many precious jewels in our hands and return to our lives. If we bury these treasures,

---

11 For a more detailed exploration of the theme of integration you may wish to read my book *San Pedro/Huachuma: Opening the Pathways of the Heart*, Las Vegas, Lifestyle Entrepreneurs Press, 2017.

they will not be of much use and they will be soon forgotten. Information alone is not power: the use of such knowledge is what really empowers us. How we translate the teachings and lessons received by the medicine can be enticing or daunting, depending on our willingness to change.

Yes, Ayahuasca can be a vehicle of rapid transformation, but it is not a quick fix that frees us from all responsibilities; on the contrary it forces us to take all the necessary steps, in thought and action, towards the full manifestation of the visions and insights we have received. Returning to unconsciousness, denial, and inertia is a possibility, but it takes even more effort than moving on and doing the things one knows are best for oneself. Full integration takes some courage, honesty, and creativity, but it is a realistic and achievable goal. One of the clearest and most useful lessons I have received from this medicine in this regard is to align all thoughts and actions when pursuing anything. The application of this very simple and logical idea has proven to be highly effective and beneficial in my life.

Asking Ayahuasca for guidance can be tricky as one should be prepared to follow that advice with as little reticence as possible: we are masters at giving advice but perform much more poorly when we have to follow it. Sometimes the change is so radical that it can be scary or seem simply impossible. Being able to capture the essence of the medicine's teachings and creating manageable goals for oneself is in the end better than dismissing the insights altogether. Such insights are often simply our own inner wisdom being allowed to resurface and be heard: to follow one's heart is the first step towards personal integrity and happiness.

Ultimately, the treasures Ayahuasca helps us rediscover are seeds that were always inside ourselves but remained locked away from our awareness. Once rediscovered and brought back to light, it is up to us to decide what we want to do with those seeds: whether we want to put them in fertile soil and tend to them so they can grow and bear fruit or not. Sometimes we may end up forgetting to take care of those seedlings to the point that they once again wither, but there is no need to worry because these seeds are the essence of our being and they are eternal and always ready to blossom once we start nurturing them again.

I always recommend people to put down in writing the insights they have received from the experience with the medicine, not just during the ceremony itself but throughout the entire process. At times these insights may come also from another person's experience that resonated deeply with us. This is an excellent way to help the conscious awareness remember the gifts we have received when we feel lost and confused. Just trust that the experience is deeply rooted inside of you no matter how far you think you may have fallen from the initial feeling of elation when you first reconnected with your deeper truths during or right after a ceremony. Paying attention to one's dreams is also a good thing as the medicine keeps working with us on that level long after its actual ingestion.

It is advisable to wait some time after the ceremonies before taking any radical decision, such as a divorce, or making an important communication to others: time allows us to see things in a better perspective and act more carefully and effectively. Also, it's important to remain aware that transformation happens first on an individual level, and that we cannot expect others to follow us down a new path they may not be ready for. On the other hand, allowing ourselves to follow our hearts automatically gives other people permission, space, and support to do the same. When our transformation is real and manifests on all levels, the world around us changes as well, perhaps not according to our ego-centered wishes and agendas but in accordance to the greater good of all. For all these reasons it is recommended to pay particular attention to oneself and whatever feelings or thought patterns that may resurface in the aftermath of the work with Ayahuasca.

Providing some time off for yourself, free of responsibilities, as well as adhering to the same dietary restrictions applied before the ceremonies may greatly facilitate the integration process. Like all matters of the spirit, such integration takes the time that it takes and shouldn't be hurried – it happens in its own time.

As part of the integration process we may unconsciously recreate familiar patterns in order to see whether our transformation is real: this is not per se a sign that things haven't been healed, but an opportunity to act differently regarding old issues, whether we choose to give in to inertia and familiar patterns, or act creatively and according to our newly found insights. At other times some important issues that we thought had been dealt with already, such as our relationship with our families, may resurface. This is not necessarily a sign that all the work up to then had been pointless and a reason for discouragement, but a chance to look at these issues from our present state of being. As we rise in consciousness, some aspects of our existence that were previously hidden or impossible to deal with, reappear for us to heal on a deeper level.

It is not uncommon that people who have done a great deal of healing work regarding certain issues are totally surprised to see those very same issues resurface in their work with Ayahuasca. Was the previous healing just make-believe or a waste of time? Not really, it's just that deeper layers of certain wounds are finally making their way to our conscious awareness to be healed and let go of.

Over the years the issues connected at first with growing up with my younger brother have resurfaced many times. This has been very challenging because often my first reaction was to blame anybody and everybody before I would start taking responsibility for how I felt. All too easily would I tend to resent this or that person for "ruining my peace of mind" until eventually it became clear that these people were only helping me see something transparent or misunderstood. But at first I would just get really upset about having to revisit stories and dynamics I have had to stare at many times before! The good part is that it becomes easier to avoid blaming others when we become aware that we play out the same little dramas but with different characters. At this point it becomes clear that these stories are not so much about other people but about ourselves, and that the only way to avoid repeating the same scenarios is to be willing to learn the lessons we try to teach ourselves once and for all.

SPIRITUAL AND PHYSICAL HEALING

Many people come to Ayahuasca in search of physical healing, often after Western medicine or other therapeutic modalities have proven to be ineffective. If one believes that physical ailments are somehow the expression of spiritual disease, then to heal that disease at its root, i.e., at the level of spirit, should result automatically in physical healing. However, in this equation there are a couple of important points to remember.

First, it is important to acknowledge how truly one believes that such healing is possible. What one wishes to believe and what one truly believes are often two very different things, and, yes, the power of the mind, whether conscious or unconscious, is nothing to be underestimated. If one truly believes that a certain healer or medicine, allopathic or other, is capable of healing, and that one is ready to accept such healing, then healing will most likely happen. Miracles, i.e., healings that medical science is unable to explain, happen all the time. But not to everyone and not all the time, no matter how intensely one wishes for them.

In the case of Ayahuasca, many extraordinary physical healings are being reported all the time, but not for everyone. It is true that the medicine does its very best in removing all sorts of toxins and pathogens, and that often people have very specific experiences of being healed on a systemic, cellular, and even genetic level. Ayahuasca's action on the physical body is a cleansing of toxins located in the physical body. Often these toxins are the physical manifestation of heavy emotions and thought patterns that have been with us for so long that they eventually take on a physical form – and often end up in being the cause of many diseases. Whether this medicine succeeds in removing the illness altogether is often a matter of how advanced that illness is.

Let's take the example of two women who came to me for a ceremony a few years ago: both of them had been diagnosed with ovarian cysts. Two weeks later one of them had a thorough medical examination, which revealed that all cysts had disappeared, whereas the other woman, even though she had received great healing and had felt that her physical issues had been resolved, found out three months later that the cysts were still there and that medical surgery was indeed needed to remove them. Had the second woman been the victim of a hallucination or of excessive wishful thinking? My personal feeling is that those cysts were already too heavily set for a full physical healing to happen, but also I believe that, if indeed the causes underlying this condition have been resolved, the chances that such cysts reappear after surgery are very slim.

I do believe that pain and suffering, emotional and physical, are doorways for personal transformation and spiritual healing. Physical healing is not a condition sine qua non of spiritual healing – a person may receive all the spiritual benefits and healings resulting from an illness such as cancer, and still die from it. In the end it doesn't really matter whether one recovers from an illness or not, provided they have taken full advantage of their experience.

I understand perfectly well the desire to be free of physical pain and ailments, but to focus all our attention on the physical side is a bit like wanting all the symptoms to be treated without ever addressing the true causes of an illness. To me as a healer it is as important and beneficial to explore the circumstances and repercussions of an ailment rather than deal strictly with its most physical manifestations. An example of this comes from the case of a woman suffering from memory loss who came to me hoping to regain her memory. As we talked about her life, I discovered that these episodes of memory loss started happening after her beloved husband's death, which caused her great suffering and left her for years in a depression. When I asked her to tell me what in her opinion these memory loss episodes may symbolize, her answer was: "I don't want to revisit and remember the past because it's too painful." So in the end I recommended to this woman that she ask the medicine not just for the healing of her memory loss but also to be shown all the things she had decided she no longer wanted to remember so she could heal her pain and let it go.

The ways of the spirit cannot easily be recognized as beneficial. Often we are overwhelmed by physical suffering and death, which are not to be disregarded because even if we may see them as illusory, they still feel very real to the people affected or to those who love them. Yet, the unsung benefits of physical illness and even "untimely" death are many, such as the reconnection of friends and family long estranged, or the letting go of animosities one has held all life long, and the forgiveness that accompanies it.

Having said all this, it is always recommended that people suffering from serious medical conditions keep seeing their regular doctors in order to evaluate their condition and keep track of their healing process.

HEALING, HOLINESS, AND ENLIGHTENMENT

Spiritual, emotional, and physical healing are essentially the dissolution of the consequences of the limiting beliefs we hold in our consciousness. These limiting beliefs mask the real nature of who we are as part of Divine Creation rather than beings separated from It. At the root of these beliefs stands the dream or illusion of separation, from which we seem to be called to wake up. To awaken from this dream seems to me the ultimate goal of human life on this planet.

Planet Earth is not a perfect place, but it is definitely the best place for us to learn the lessons we have come here for as incarnated beings. Clearly we are here in order to learn and remember the truths we have somehow forgotten. The lessons we decide to learn from the dimension of Spirit often seem overwhelmingly filled with pain once we incarnate.

Our identification with our physical bodies makes these earthly experiences truly challenging as our first concerns end up being connected with survival rather than the fulfillment of these personal soul contracts.

Our immediate goals in life are connected with safety and the continuation of our species. Later in life, as we reach a certain level of psychological maturity, we long for connection and fulfilling relationships that we interpret as a way of reaching an ever-eluding state of happiness. Eventually, as we tire of this endless pursuit of happiness, we look for peace of mind and in some cases enlightenment. All of these goals are tiny steps towards the greater goal of reuniting with the Divine. Along this path we are often called to face episodes of physical illness, emotional distress, and spiritual crisis. We try as best as we can to "fix," as quickly as possible, these often-painful events in order to regain a certain sense of "normality" and be able to live our lives with ease. Disease of any kind is fiercely avoided and denied in our modern society, whereas it can be taken as an excellent opportunity to grow and fulfill the deeper purpose of our life.

The real chance of healing the separation from the Divine often assumes the form of wounds such as rejection, abandonment, and other conditions of loss and betrayal. These wounds are re-enacted as soon as we come into this world, and we seem to very skillfully choose the perfect family environment and situations to bring these issues back to the surface. Parents and siblings, who are in most cases, particularly in the first stages of our lives, blamed for the misery we find ourselves in, are actually our very first and most important teachers. As we heal and let go of these wounds we find ourselves living our lives with a greater lightness of being, compassion towards others, and love.

One of the first positive outcomes of working with this medicine is the resurfacing of gratitude, a feeling that is often connected with higher spiritual levels of being. Another one is the experience of everything being in some way interconnected and sacred. This is often the result of being able to see the inherent unity of all of Creation, seen and unseen, or, as it happened one night to me, through the revelation of the omnipresence of the Divine.

I was sitting at the beginning of a ceremony waiting for the medicine to take effect when a voice inside my head started saying, "God is everywhere." At first it was only a whisper, then a statement, until it became a proclamation that wouldn't stop. I was ecstatic but still cautious and so began to ask myself whether I really believed that God was also present in the most unlikely of places such as hospitals and garbage dumps. The answer came back always positive, and so I spent most of the ceremony deepening that experience of the sacredness of everything and everyone. The next day as I walked along a familiar road in the jungle, I looked at every tree, animal, and cloud feeling their holiness, an awareness that has stayed with me ever since.

My own personal work with Ayahuasca has brought about a radical shift in the way I see myself, others, and life on this planet. Letting go of ego-centered concerns has enabled me to live my life more fully than ever, and has opened up vibratory channels until then obstructed by the debris of the past. In this sense my own healing has been truly instrumental in the development of my spiritual path.

An unforgettable vision happened to me during my first visit to Iquitos: during a ceremony I was taken into what seemed to be the Buddhist Heaven. Upon my arrival I was greeted by Gautama Buddha, who bowed to me saying, "We have been waiting for you for a long time," and then turned to point to me an infinite landscape of clouds, upon which countless Buddhas were sitting in lotus position, and who greeted me with a gentle bow of the head. I was elated, not so much by the vision of a Buddhist Heaven, whose actual existence is of little importance to me, but by the fact that I had unknowingly been prepared for such experience by the healing work I was engaging in.

Another example comes from the experiences of a man who has been working with me lately and whose main intention in these ceremonies has been primarily to become a conduit between humans and other spiritual dimensions. This is what he wrote regarding his third and fourth ceremonies with me:

At some point these shapeshifters took me to many realms. At first it seemed easy but they said I would need to purge more and more of the heavy energy I was carrying to be able to vibrate fast enough to reach the higher realms. They knew what energy I had to purge and told me they would take care of knowing what to purge. Each place required more and more purging. I was becoming exhausted and they kept saying have you had enough? I kept saying show me more just don't kill me.

One of the most interesting places they said was where only light existed. They were helping me vibrate and kept saying vibrate faster, faster. I realized if I shorten the time between harmonics I could vibrate faster. The shaman was singing chants over me and I used the energy in the chant. The Jaguar people said you need more energy and suggested that some people use the energy of the Kundalini and it would be enough. My whole body was shaking from the Kundalini rushing into my head and suddenly a huge column of white light shot down from above me and I was in the dimension of just light. It was alive and the light was made up of crystals that were constantly moving. The energy was fantastic and almost overwhelming. I was inviting the shaman and anyone around me to share in this unlimited energy. The shaman later said he had to step back when this column of light shot down. It was so intense. The shapeshifters were taking me faster and faster to different places and as soon as I had purged they took me to another asking, "Have you had enough?" Purge, travel, purge, travel, purge, travel...

My intention for the next ceremony was to open all the gates or blockages into the higher realms of existence in order to act as a conduit for other people. The spirit guide said, "There are no closed gates into these realms. They are always open to anyone. The blockages are all in you. You don't need to search the whole Universe to find these realms. They are right in front of you. They are here on the Earth." As these people worked at my feet, I was hearing loud buzzing sounds in my head and feeling surges of electrical currents and light flooding into my spine. The work seemed to go on for over an hour. Then, one of them said, "Try activating your Kundalini, now." As I made the familiar effort, the Kundalini came with tremendous force and ease. It was like the channel had been cleared and the force came without any resistance.

The spirit guide told me the force should be "sipped" and not drank. He said my ability to "see" would be gradually increasing. It would be very confusing to open this ability too fast. There was a very thin veil that he would remove in my perception to allow this process to begin. As he removed this veil, I first saw my wife as a little girl holding a doll, and then I saw her as older, maybe 11 or 12. I could feel her happy emotions. Then I saw her as she was entering puberty. The changes in her body, the new powers of womanhood were confusing for her. Her relationship in the world as a teen seemed to be cast alone into a tempest without any guidance. This lack of adjustment lasted well into her future. She had been the child of alcoholics and had brought this up many times in our long relationship as the cause of many of her problems. I could "see" this adjustment to adolescence was the beginning of these issues and not the case of blaming things on her parents without assuming any responsibility herself.

In these ceremonies this man experienced all sorts of cleansings, from physical and energetic to the removal of "veils" in his perception and consciousness that were experienced as barriers to the furthering of his spiritual path. With these purifications came also greater awareness and an increased ability to see beyond appearances. It is not uncommon that those on a spiritual path develop along the way special gifts such as clairvoyance and the ability to heal others. These are by-products and not the end-of-it-all of the spiritual quest, and in many cases they present just another opportunity to test the fortitude and integrity of the seeker. Beyond all psychic abilities and "powers," when one doesn't get attached to them but at best shares them for the benefit of all, lies the land of mystical and eternal reunion with the Divine, called "salvation" by some and "enlightenment" by others.

It is written in "*Supplements to A Course in Miracles*"[12] that the only part of ourselves that needs healing is our minds, as our minds are what create separation and therefore suffering. As all creations of the mind are ultimately illusions, then Ayahuasca, and all therapeutic modalities, are illusory medicines for illusory problems. Their power lies in making us aware of the illusion and supporting us in letting it go so that we can embrace the deeper reality of our eternal and divine essence.

The use of Ayahuasca as a medicine for the soul can indeed help us move closer to the Divine. In many cultures there is an ingrained diffidence towards the use of entheogens for spiritual purposes, and indeed this is a path that holds many dangers and challenges, just like any spiritual path. Perhaps the greatest gift and danger lies in the speed at which transformation can occur when working with Ayahuasca. When working with the man whose experiences were related beforehand, my main concern was that he could benefit from it all without being overwhelmed by it. Sudden and big shifts in consciousness can simply short-circuit anyone who isn't fully prepared to receive them, which is why this work requires great discipline and patience. The spiritual path is hardly ever a straight line from A to B but often a winding road along peak and valleys – at times this is source of discouragement and a test of our determination: perseverance, trust,

---

12   Supplements to A Course in Miracles, Foundation for Inner Peace, Viking Penguin, 1996.

and faith are our best allies when hope starts running low.

Some people with a long history of spiritual search may find that working with Ayahuasca brings back all sorts of teachings that were until then somewhat believed in but never truly experienced as valid. This medicine sometimes stresses the divide between theory and actual experience, but also helps us leap across it. We can read about apples and enlightenment for lifetimes, but only sinking our teeth into them will satisfy our longing. It is said in Peru that patience is the science of peace, and Gautama Buddha is quoted as having said that once we hear of enlightenment there is nothing else we could possibly want. The vow of countless Bodhisattvas not to enter Heaven until all of us are in it seems to me all the proof needed to know that enlightenment or salvation are unavoidable and just a matter of time, a time which loses all relevance in the wake of Eternity. So, while we are here on this journey we may as well make the most of it and enjoy the company of our soul brothers and sisters who have had the courage to sign up for this amazing adventure.

The temporary dissolution of the ego under the effects of Ayahuasca and the resulting ecstasy we experience when the rational mind is quiet give us glimpses of our real nature as spiritual beings. These experiences show us who we really are behind all appearances and help us embody our true divinity and spiritual essence while still living on this planet.

My own personal experience of enlightenment, or rather self-realization, came at the end of a quite dramatic personal crisis that led me to undertake a few recent solo ceremonies in order to deal with the issues that once again had come up for me – issues

I had dealt with repeatedly over the years but had clearly not been quite resolved completely. The final healing of some deep wounds and the resulting letting go of some childhood drama brought me to a spontaneous realization that the healing I had been seeking for years had finally happened. The resulting inner peace mixed with elation is difficult to describe, but what was clear was a sense of letting go of all inner conflicts and pretense. Rather than feeling as if I had achieved something, I felt myself relaxing into my true nature and being. In the days following this experience I noticed during one of my walks that I was indeed experiencing this Universe without the veil of fear and judgment that had clouded my entire life: walking on this beautiful Earth in complete peace allowed me to finally experience its quiet majesty, its amazing Life force, and the blessing of being part of it all. At some point I felt the wheel of reincarnation coming to a stop: it wasn't just the absence of desire, but also the absence of fear that made this dynamic come to a halt. I believe that in this world of duality every action and thought is not only caused by desire but by fear as well: letting go of all fear led me to a state devoid of desire as well. When my deeply held unconscious fear of Divine Love was gone, I was finally able to bask in It limitlessly and beyond time itself. With such total fulfillment, all personal desires had no reason to be and simply subsided. In that moment I felt free from the chains of unconscious birth and rebirth – light and fully present. I have no idea how permanent this awareness will be with me in this lifetime, but I now know this to be the very nature of who we are as part of Divine Creation.

In order to ground myself, as soon as I got back home I simply went ahead and watered my garden remembering the old Zen story of the monk who goes back to the well to fetch water after reaching enlightenment: life continues just as it did before but with a new and deep awareness that is undeniable and always present in every moment.

The identity of the spiritual seeker had to be eventually let go of and simply replaced by the acceptance of my true nature, without doubt and without hesitation. I then could look at the world reflecting back to me the inner light and unconditional love I was experiencing.

In retrospect I can see how all the spiritual literature I had been reading since my adolescence had certainly opened the way for me and yet had kept the final goal somehow out of reach. The stories I had been reading had made the experience of enlightenment seem like the privilege of a fortunate few. Now I know this state to be the birthright of absolutely everyone.

Part III

"Hanan Pacha" by Harry Chavez, 2010

SHAMANIC DIETS

November, 2011
I am on a slow boat to Tamanco, Don Francisco's native village two days away on the Ucayali river, somewhere between Iquitos and Pucallpa.

It's been five years (already?) since my last diet in the jungle. I am looking forward to a full month in the middle of nowhere in the Amazon jungle with my teacher and a group of ten friends. The long boat trip helps me gently let go of the stress accumulated in the last few weeks. The blue sky stretches into infinity as we make our way upstream. By the time we arrive at our final destination we all feel pretty mellow and once settled in my hut at the end of the simple settlement that will be our home for the next four weeks, I proceed to do as little as possible (and often nothing at all). Leaving Iquitos two days earlier I had had my last cigarette: I am here also to give up smoking, which I have indulged in for way too long.

I am happy to spend most of my days and nights under the mosquito net on my bed, looking out into the surrounding jungle through a thin layer of fabric. The sounds of the forest and the sky turn into a strong yet soothing music that is ever present and sublime. I fill my entire being with the peace, the beauty, and the vibrations of this land and spend most of my waking hours simply inhaling and exhaling, inhaling and exhaling.

Usually a month-long diet would be a cause of trepidation and a bit of anxiety at the prospect of having so much time to myself and the impossibility of running from myself in the usual ways. But not this time – I am actually looking forward to it. I brought no entertainment and need none: I am perfectly content doing absolutely nothing. In the absence of activity I cannot help connecting with my surroundings and listening to it.

In a short time I notice that the jungle, which is often thought of as a hostile and only-the-strong-can-survive environment, is actually truly harmonious: a space where each element is naturally part of a whole that thrives perfectly well just as is.

I begin to see on a large and living 3-D scale a manifestation of creative order and balance. I can feel that what is labeled by many as "the cruel law of jungle survival" is just the way things are: perfectly natural. I realize that just by being in such a large well-balanced eco-system I will be mending torn parts of my body and mind. The absence of conflict outside me is a state of being that keeps seeping in as the days progress. And then, in this beautiful and nourishing cocoon I can start dealing as gracefully as possible with whatever the diet process will bring up for me at this time in my life as I, without smoking, explore the themes of addiction, repressed rage and hatred, vulnerability, trust, and betrayal.

For me, beside the Sacred Valley of Peru where I live, there is really no better place than the jungle to deal with my own demons and feel totally and lovingly supported by the natural environment in my process. I feel the medicine of this place, its stories, and its spirits. The jungle takes care of me as one of her many children and I am happy to visit a few rooms of my own personal hell while being held in her loving arms. I do not feel threatened – I feel loved and deeply cared for.

The theme of privilege came up soon, already in Iquitos, with my fellow dieteros. Despite the absence of most comforts, to me being able to enjoy time in the jungle in a diet is a real privilege. To benefit personally from a wealth of wisdom unknown to most of the rest of humanity is a deeply appreciated gift and blessing. That I may go through the pangs of hunger and temporary bouts of mild schizophrenia is a small price I am willing to pay for the benefits I always receive from a diet in the jungle.

To be able to be in my teacher's loving presence and expert guidance, guest of a people and land I had never even contemplated visiting in this lifetime: yes, all of this is a real privilege.

After my first 12-day diet in Peru in 2004, I used to go around telling people how sincerely I believed that if all humans went through that same experience at least once in their lives, life on this planet would be a totally different story. Part of me still fancies that idea.

I have engaged in many kinds of spiritual and healing processes but have found none as profound as a shamanic plant diet with the right medicines and under the proper supervision. The power of this process is so strong that I am affected by it even when I lead a diet for someone else without being in a diet myself.

And here I am again for a month-long diet. Having been in different places in the Peruvian Amazon I am very pleasantly surprised by the entire setting and Don Francisco is happily on top of his game.

The first time I was in the jungle I was amazed by the fact that here was a group of foreigners, descendants like myself of those very Spanish who did terrible things in the past to these natives, not least of all try to destroy their ancestral wisdom and traditions. I was amazed that here we were, 500 years later, asking to be healed in the same ways we had demonized centuries earlier. I was amazed that that wisdom had not been destroyed as the Conquistadores would have wished, but that it's alive and that the natives are open-minded and openhearted enough to share this wisdom with whoever is willing to receive it and benefit from it. What a privilege.

So I make the most of my time in the jungle, being as present to myself as I can. Not afraid of the jungle, just in awe of it. And in trust and surrender.

Ayahuasca is not the only healing plant of the Amazon jungle – there are countless other species used for all sorts of illnesses of the body and the spirit. The process used for working with different plants is known as "la dieta" or "shamanic diet," and it is basically the same whether it is for personal healing, interest and development, or a shamanic apprenticeship.

The diet requires stricter restrictions than those involved with drinking Ayahuasca. During a diet one abstains from salt, sugar, spices, fatty foods, and pork, as well as alcohol, caffeine, and other mind-altering substances. Usually meals consist of white rice, plantains, manioc, potatoes, vegetables, eggs, and occasionally fish and meat.[13] It is not a rich diet, and after a while the physical body feels clear of toxins but weakened, and physical efforts are reduced to a minimum. Moreover one abstains from sexual activities of all sorts. Last but not least, the "dietero" lives in relative to absolute seclusion, avoiding casual contact and communication with others.

The principle behind these restrictions is similar to the one used by Hindu, Buddhist, or Taoist spiritual seekers, and they are enforced to limit distractions from the physical world and stimuli, so that one can better focus on the subtler energies of the spirit. Inputs from the outside, such as foods, tastes, colors, shapes, music, and noises, keep our attention constantly projected onto the outside and saturate our perception with sensory stimuli to the point of clogging our ability to see and feel the more subtle aspects of Life. By reducing these inputs the "dietero" can create a space where these energies can be experienced and their messages heard. What is heard at first, as is the case in the beginning of a meditation practice, is the constant chattering away of the mind. After that the emotions and dynamics held at bay by constant distractions and suppression start making their appearance so they can be healed, a process that is also catalyzed by the plants one is working with.

The purification of the body and the mind, the quiet surroundings, and the lack of activities help shift the awareness towards the subtler ways of the spirit: the dialogue between conscious awareness and the

---

13 The foods served at retreat centers in the Amazon vary from place to place and can range, within the mentioned parameters from really basic to more diverse.

soul is then more clearly perceived, and its meanings more clearly understood. The quiet voice of intuition can finally be listened to and acknowledged: insights make their appearance spontaneously during the waking state as well as in dreams.

The goal of a diet is to connect energetically and spiritually with other plants, and receive their healing, guidance, and gifts. This process is unlike anything assumed as valid in modern cultures, and for a reason, as it totally bypasses the rational component of human activity. The question is whether we believe ourselves to be exclusively the sum of our rational brain activities. Just the awareness that our bodily functions happen totally on their own even in deep sleep should shake even the most skeptic from the assumption that the conscious mind is everything. Once liberated from the tight constraints of the materialistic and rational view of the world, one is free to explore all the other levels of the human experience without prejudice: the heart, intuition, extrasensory perception (ESP), the soul, and the spirit. It is at these levels and vibrations that the diet's most profound effects take place, and it is at these levels that one is invited to resonate in order to become aware of what is happening.

During my several diets what I experienced varied according to my needs and wishes, my sensitivity to the process, and the specific plants I was working with. After four months of dieting the Datura plant, my teacher suggested I work with the Tobacco plant, primarily in order to ground me. I was very astonished to see how by this simple process the plant not only brought me back into my body but also taught me how to work with it without any clear instruction but in a totally intuitive and non-verbal way.

In the case of my work with Chiric Sanango (*Brunfelsia uniflora*), which I was dieting in order to balance my attitude towards cold weather, I was surprised to see how this plant was helping me on more levels than just the physical one by dissipating a level of emotional coldness I had not even been aware of. Later on I decided to work with the Rose plant in order to be able to better help others in their issues with the Feminine: as it is usually the case, this learning process happened by experiencing first-hand the healing properties of this plant. I was confronted with the wounds I was carrying from my mother's lineage, and in particular the anger that had resulted in my grandmother's premature death. This process turned out to be particularly challenging and after four weeks I had to interrupt the diet because of the overwhelming feelings I was connecting with. But it was a good start and a year later I was finally able to grieve my grandmother, almost forty years after her death.

In the course of a diet the "dietero" will be drinking decoctions and teas made from the chosen plants, according to one's needs and the plants' mode of use. Some shamans work with specific plants and will propose them to those interested in this process; others, as in the case of my teacher, connect with plant spirits in order to find out which plant wants or is best suited to work with a specific person. In my case it was a bit of both: there were plants that I was interested in working with, others that were suggested by my teacher, and others that came to me such as with the Datura plant or Remo Caspi (*Aspidosperma excelsum*). This latter appeared to me during an Ayahuasca ceremony as a large but unfamiliar tree. When I told my teacher about this vision he suggested I go around the jungle looking for it. After visiting another tree, which I thought might be the one but wasn't, I saw a specimen of Remo Caspi and instinctively knew that my search was over and a week later started working with it.

The diet process is not to be taken lightly, and should be undertaken only with the expert supervision and guidance of an experienced shaman. Working with a single plant or more plants at the same time can take anywhere from two weeks to several months. To those people not native of the Amazon region I would not recommend engaging in diets longer than two months at a time and to allow enough time in between for the physical body to recuperate its strength. In my hurry to learn as quickly as possible I made the mistake of dieting intensely for one year over the period of two years and ended up with serious metabolic dysfunctions as a result of the poor diet and the frequent diarrhea and vomit induced by drinking Ayahuasca three times a week for such a long period of time. I hope my own story can serve as a good cautionary tale to even the most enthusiastic.

The dieta is a long process designed to calm the mind and allow us to hear and feel what is ordinarily out of reach in our regular state of awareness. The connection with these plants is at the same time physical and spiritual, and varies according to one's openness and willingness to engage in the process. Once again it is not just about receiving gifts from these plants, but about what we are willing and ready to give (or give up) in order to take part in the process. Each plant has its own qualities and gifts: some are particularly effective in healing physical ailments, others are useful in cleansing the spirit of heavy energies, others can be powerful guides in the realms of the spirit. The experience can be that of a deep connection with other beings, in this case plants or plant spirits, or, as it has been my experience, that of being mirrored by these Plant Teachers aspects of my own self until then sub- or unconscious. The qualities and wisdom of these plants are not otherworldly but part of our own heritage as divine beings. Over the years what has been transmitted to me by these teachers has never clashed against my own highest beliefs but has simply provided a deepening and experience of such beliefs.

Often, but not necessarily, a diet is combined with the drinking of Ayahuasca, which is then called "the Mother of all Plants" in that it allows us to enter in contact with the energies and spirits of all the other plants, to discern their use, and receive their guidance. The expansion of consciousness provided by Ayahuasca lets us see and feel what could otherwise remain invisible and inaccessible. Ayahuasca is then not only a healer in its own right, but also opens the connection between humans and all the other energies of the Universe.

As with the work with Ayahuasca, the diet process is likely to be challenging, physically, psychologically, and spiritually, and should be engaged in only by the most willing and determined. Life in the jungle can be challenging in and of itself for people unused to it. The living conditions in the places where one can do a diet are often devoid of comforts such as electricity, warm water, or easy access to "civilization." One is usually given a simple hut ("tambo") with a bed and mosquito net, and basic furniture like a table and stool, a hammock, and candles. Conventional toilets and bathing facilities are a luxury. Traditionally, natives have little use for books, which get easily damaged by mold or eaten by termites, and in some cases reading and listening to pre-recorded music is frowned upon. If books and music are accepted, it is recommended that one chooses inspirational material rather than, say, detective stories, romantic novels, or heavy metal music.

The dietary restrictions are the most difficult to endure, particularly when one has little other distractions: this is a yoga, a discipline of purification of the mind and the spirit, during which all of our demons, fears, and neuroses are likely to resurface.

In addition to all this, we must face and come to terms with a natural surrounding that is very powerful and healing, but that can also be perceived as threatening: heat, extreme humidity, torrential rains, snakes, spiders, insects of all shapes and sizes capable of making their way into everything, mosquitoes constantly looking for food - and nowhere to run to, or take shelter, except under a mosquito net well tucked and without holes. The romantic ideal of a visit to the Amazon jungle can be quickly destroyed by the reality of a harsh environment, which should not be underestimated.

I was personally blessed upon my first visit to the jungle for a diet by the almost total absence of mosquitoes. All of us participants had been warned about the challenges we might encounter but I was delighted to be in what seemed like Heaven on Earth. Even so, it only took a couple of days before I complained to our guide about the dreadfully poor diet we had to endure. He must have heard similar complaints many times before and simply listened to me with patience and a smile. During other visits to the jungle the situation with the mosquitoes had me spend most of my time under my mosquito net – my only solution at hand.

It is important that people take whatever precautions necessary, particularly regarding mosquito-borne infections. While prophylaxis against malaria is highly toxic and not recommended, it is important to minimize mosquito bites as much as possible, with appropriate clothing and DEET-containing lotions if necessary. The rainy season, which in the Peruvian Amazon lasts from December until April, is the time of highest mosquito activity, and incidence of malaria and dengue fever outbreaks. Nonetheless, with the right attitude and flexibility, life in the jungle can be a most amazing experience: the Life energy, manifesting itself through myriads of animal and plants in endless variations, is deeply felt as healing, tonic, and regenerating. The fact of being in the diet process greatly enhances our ability to connect with this Life force and benefit from it. The slow pace of a life devoid of distractions can be maddening at times, but when we stop resisting and start flowing with it, it becomes the greatest of medicines: the rhythm of Nature gently restores our internal clock, often out of tune because of the stress of our daily lives. Nature starts speaking to us because we are more open to listen to it: it shares its stories and myths, its secrets and mysteries. Everything takes on a deeper meaning: we are no longer in a rational space of clearly defined causes and effects, but enter the realms of magic, where the Great Mystery need not be solved but simply embraced.

The group dynamics we can encounter during an Ayahuasca ceremony can of course be easily played out during a diet. In the best of cases the diet will help bring awareness and healing to these patterns.

I remind everybody, including myself, that we are all teachers to one another. When we mirror to one another images that are far from stellar, usually conflict ensues. Reminding ourselves that what we see in others are only aspects of ourselves is the quickest way out of the projections' maze of our lives.

I also strongly discourage everybody from entertaining romantic thoughts and fantasies that involve other people present during a diet. Falling in love with a stranger while on a diet can be more confusing than anything else but, when we sit back instead of acting upon it, can also lead us to deeper awareness, interesting discoveries, and great healing. I fell in love with someone the first time I went to the jungle but after 48 hours of obsessive thinking I realized I was distracting myself from the real purpose of my visit and quickly let go of my romantic musings altogether.

By the way, couples can participate in a diet together but should give themselves enough time and space for their own individual experience as well.

The shamanic plant diet process can also be applied to healing stones. This is usually done by soaking the stones and crystals in water and then drinking the water that received the vibrations of the minerals. The "dieta" is also a valid model for connecting to plants and minerals all over the world, and can be used to approach these in a shamanic fashion wherever we are, not just in the Amazon jungle. Extensive practice under the watchful eye of an expert shaman is necessary before anyone tries this alone at home, and particular care and attention must be exercised when dealing with plants and rocks that are unfamiliar: guidance, caution, intuition, and meditation are the best tools to safely navigate these realms.

SORCERY AND BLACK MAGIC:

THE DARK SIDE OF SHAMANISM

The subject of sorcery and black magic is a sensitive one. For many Westerners sorcery is met with disbelief; however in South America and in many traditional societies all over the world it is a reality, and therefore worth examining whether one believes in its existence or not.

Black magic encompasses all actions made with the intention of hurting or weakening others, and includes also those actions carried out without their explicit consent, even when it is believed to be "for their own good." To this list of actions I would also add the taking advantage of someone's position of authority, i.e., the healer, in order to manipulate others to their own advantage.

The execution of sorcery is the realm of shamans and sorcerers: people ask for their help in order to hurt others because of jealousy, envy, or other emotional states. The role of the shaman is closely related to that of a doctor, and in general doctors are ethically forbidden to hurt other human beings. This is not always the case: there are shamans who think nothing of using their power to hurt and even kill people if adequately paid for their services. They usually accomplish this by sending invisible darts ("virotes") to their clients' enemies, by magically having their victims fall prey to poisonous animals or plants, or by causing them to have serious accidents. The result is often an inexplicable and sometimes lethal illness that can be healed only by another shaman of equal or superior power.

Sometimes these shamanic attacks can take place during an Ayahuasca ceremony: anyone who feels attacked by an exterior energy should share this information with the guide as soon as possible in order to neutralize the negative effects of such occurrence.

Sometimes it is the very guide who is abusing his or her power and position to hurt someone in attendance: in such rare cases one would do best to leave the ceremony discretely and look for a safe place to go. This is often impossible as ceremonies happen at night in secluded places – if that's the case one can protect oneself as much as possible by surrounding oneself with a protective vibration, an energetic shield to fend off the attack. The same procedure is effective against any other kind of weird vibrations that may appear during a ceremony, whether from the guide, the ceremonial space, or other participants. Overreacting to these attacks only makes us more vulnerable – the best attitude is to patiently and silently wait until the end of the ceremony.

I had such an incident happen to me during a ceremony in the jungle with my teacher. I was sitting next to someone who unbeknownst to me was suffering from some sort of black magic attack. From early on I felt uneasy sitting where I was and ended up leaving the ceremony after asking my teacher for the permission to do so. (It may be said that leaving a ceremony alone before it's closed is usually not a good idea but it made perfect sense to me that night.) The uneasiness persisted for the next two days until I decided to take a bath with the plant Aya Uma (*Couroupita sp.*), which had been useful to me in the past to clear some particularly dark energies. After the bath I felt much better and eventually discovered that the person I had sat next to in the previous ceremony had been attacked by another shaman and that what I had felt was most likely the dark energies attached to this man. As a result of this attack he was trying to kill himself and refused to receive the care of a tabaquero, who was trying to get this spell out of him, which to me indicated the work of a very powerful and skilled sorcerer.

Furthermore, one should pay particular attention to the source of these dark energies: in the majority of occurrences, these are actually no other than one's own darkness resurfacing, which is sometimes difficult to own and more easily projected onto others.

Shamans acquire their powers through shamanic diets, during which they receive the powers of plants and trees, or by invoking particular cosmic energies. These powers are generally neutral and can be used to do either good or bad: it is up to each individual to decide for what purpose they want to apply them. Medicine people easily seduced by money, sex, or power, can be overcome by the acquisition of these supernatural powers, and can end up using them not to heal but to hurt others. The seduction of power is a trial every shaman needs to confront sooner or later (and a recurring theme for people who drink Ayahuasca or engage in shamanic diets and practices), the outcome of which will determine whether one is a white or a black magician.

The first time I became aware of the gifts and "powers" I was receiving from a plant during a diet process I felt intoxicated by the feeling of great power. It had a dizzying effect, from which I eventually managed to get out instead of falling into it. All of this happened without warning or introduction and only when it was over did I fully realize that temptation had knocked hard at my door.

The distinction between a white and a black sorcerer is not always clear as a self-proclaimed healer can at any time be assailed by jealousy, hatred, or a sense that he or she is above the moral law of his people. This is something that happens to all humans, and we have all been guilty on more than one occasion of wishing others less than the best. The problem gets worse when the wish to hurt others is acted upon and it is someone with special powers that carries it out.

Sorcerers are people that despite their powers vibrate at a low level of consciousness, and it is at this level that they operate, always hitting their victims where they are most vulnerable, taking advantage of their weaknesses, be they physical, moral, or spiritual. In this sense those who try to hurt us can become powerful teachers because they point their attacks where we are weakest, thus showing us our shortcomings and blind spots. The Sufis say that our enemies are just the shadow we cast. Black sorcerers can point out to us these shadows we have been reluctant to acknowledge thus far.

I was personally attacked by other medicine people on two separate occasions in 2011. In both instances I was accused of being a dangerous black sorcerer because of my choice to work not only with Ayahuasca but also with the San Pedro cactus. Working with both of these Master Plants is not a popular choice but no reason for such accusations, which were unfounded and clearly meant to destabilize me. It was very painful, but by the second attack, as I was listening to this person's accusations, I realized that what I was being shown was a reflection of my own ways of asserting spiritual or moral superiority over others. I could finally see in broad daylight the ugliness and stupidity of the Inquisition and of all religious and racial conflict that have ever happened. Seeing this whole picture with such clarity allowed me not only to forgive my attackers but also forgive myself for all those instances when I had fallen prey to believing I was superior or inferior to others and the pain I had both inflicted and suffered over lifetimes because of this belief.

A white magician on the other hand is someone dedicated to helping others heal and come into their own power. So, before associating oneself with any shaman or guide, it is very important that one gets a clear feeling that the prospective guide is one who is first and foremost dedicated to healing and not motivated by, nor attached to money, sex, or power. In this regard, it helps greatly not to engage with the shaman either sexually or romantically in any way, and not to make any promises of financial help one isn't going to fulfill: a smitten person can become very dangerous!

It doesn't hurt to ask ourselves whether our interest in shamanic practices is motivated by a desire to make ourselves more interesting, seductive, and powerful for selfish reasons. At least once a year I take the time to renew what I refer to as "my vows of service to the medicine." This is a time for expressing gratitude for all the blessings this medicine has bestowed upon me and those who come to me for healing, and it's also a time for earnest introspection. I ask myself what my actual reasons for leading ceremonies have been. I started doing this periodically after a friend was found dead in his apartment and another ended up in a psychiatric hospital. I believe black magic was one of the key reasons for their misfortunes and so I probed myself deeply inside myself to see if there were any vulnerable spots where I could be hurt. I intuitively understood that someone trying to attack me would be operating from a lower charkas perspective and therefore I would be most vulnerable in the lower charkas as well. So every few months I ask myself whether I am operating consciously or unconsciously out of a desire for money, sex, or power. If I did, then I believe I would have plenty of good reasons to fear a black magic attack from other people vibrating at these same levels.

Traditionally powerful knowledge and practices would be transmitted only after many years of low level apprenticeship, during which the master would assess the moral aptitude of the student to receive certain teachings. Nowadays the availability of such knowledge is radically greater, but that doesn't mean that it has become any less dangerous in the hands of someone with ambiguous or downright bad intentions.

Despite the popularity of sorcery, Peru is still full of shamans and medicine people of great integrity and wisdom. Charlatans abound just like in any other profession: it is up to us to decide whether we want to be fooled and abused, or not. Sometimes such power of decision and deliberation is clouded by old dynamics that despite our best efforts drive us back into situations that can become uncomfortable or dangerous. People with a tendency to be disappointed or taken advantage of by others, or have a history of abuse or self-sabotage, are advised to take particular care of the choices they make in order to avoid the recurrence of such patterns, and instead find people that can help them understand and heal.

A young woman I met recently was not as lucky: she had been in a serious car accident and her partner had recommended a shaman in Peru to help her heal the physical wounds that she had suffered. When she arrived in the jungle she paid in advance for a month-long stay. To her surprise the shaman was already quite old and would easily doze off in the middle of the Ayahuasca ceremonies, so much so that after a while she was put in the care of one of the shaman's apprentices. When I met her she was beside herself and kept talking about the dark energies and questionable behaviors she had encountered there: it turned out that the shaman's apprentice and her ended up engaging in sexual activities, once even right after the end of a ceremony. The relationship grew even more difficult when this apprentice started having sex with other guests as well. When I asked her about the circumstances of her car accident, this woman told me it happened right after she had found her boyfriend at the time with another woman and had ended the relationship because of it. Upon hearing all this I started pointing out to her how she had gone to the jungle hoping for healing and instead of gaining more clarity she had ended up recreating a similar scenario of abuse and betrayal as before but with different characters.

Unfortunately her visit to the jungle turned into the re-enactment of some very painful dynamics and resulted in more confusion and upset rather than the healing and release she had hoped for. Since her departure from the jungle she had been so busy accusing this man of so many things that she had failed to realize she had repeated the same story she had come to heal. Putting all the blame on this apprentice and expressing her bewilderment regarding his lack of integrity and evil ways, she was trying to convince herself and those around her that she had been the victim of dark forces against her will. As I was inviting her to question her version of what had happened and consider the possibility of her being somewhat responsible for it, I also pointed out to how in unexpected ways her prayers for healing had been at least partly answered: little by little she was actually making progress and understanding the reason for the anger that had caused her car accident.

Like many others I also spent the first couple of years here in Peru voicing my disappointment at the lack of integrity of certain medicine people, but have since come to believe that there are no good or evil shamans: we are all simply having the experience we need or wish to have, whether consciously or unconsciously. Expecting other people to be free from all greed and lust just because we think of them as spiritual guides of some sort is upon closer inspection a little farfetched, and it's an assumption that has been proved over and over to be unrealistic. The truth of the matter is that as long as we need to have the experience of being abused and hurt, we shall have no short supply of people willing to abuse and hurt us. Even swamis, high priests of any religion, and shamans.

AYAHUASCA AND
THE FEMININE

There is much talk these days about a supposed shift in the spiritual center of the world, which for thousands of years was reputed to be around the Himalayas. This shift seems to be associated with an evolutionary need to reconnect with the Feminine in all its aspects. The South American Andes and its neighboring Amazon region have been attracting large numbers of spiritual seekers from all over the world in the past couple of decades and the main reason seems to be the particularly feminine qualities of this land, which is referred to as "Pachamama," i.e., "Mother Earth." Indeed this land is a powerful and nurturing Mother, ready to support and guide us in every step of our path, and it is no coincidence that the spiritual practices of this part of the world, which are connected not only to Spirit but also to Nature, are enjoying great popularity worldwide.

Since the dawn of time women have been the natural keepers of Nature's mysteries and wisdom.

While hunting was a male occupation, food gathering and later on agriculture has always been more of a female task. The female connection with the Earth has therefore been very strong, on the one hand because of women gathering food and learning about plants, and also because of the intrinsic identity between women and Nature as life givers. The procreative quality of women most closely resembles that of the Earth, hence the universal view of our planet as Mother Earth. Unfortunately such primordial connection between women and Nature has been eroded by many centuries of patriarchal rule, which has had the effect of disempowering women by controlling and limiting the exercise of their natural gifts.

The shift from Nature-based religious practices and the demonizing of the powers of Nature are both aspects of the evolution of mankind towards a male-dominated society and a psychic universe where the female principle is repressed in favor of more masculine energies such as the rational mind, science, control, and aggression. This evolutionary process hasn't happened by accident but corresponds to a need to explore the male aspect of our intrinsic polarity as human beings. Today we find ourselves at the very peak of such exploration, in a world that unfortunately feels more and more out of balance between these two principles, and where the excessive power given to male energy, so intent on controlling and seeing the Earth only in terms of material resources to be exploited, is threatening the very survival of our species on the planet.

The way our culture treats Nature and women is one and the same, and women have been banned from naturally contributing to civilization, and usually allowed to occupy only a place of subservience. The plight of women doesn't concern only women but all of society and the entire planet: as the other half of who we are, physically, psychologically, symbolically, and spiritually, their oppression carries consequences for everybody, whether we are aware of it or not. Of course the first ones to suffer from the phobia of the Feminine are women. The systematic discrimination many may feel from early childhood makes even the strongest individual female question her gender identity at one point or another. The modern fight for equal rights between men and women often results in women having to become more masculine in a male-dominated society, instead of being allowed to bring into the social structure more feminine energies and principles.

Women are aware that without their help and vision the world is at considerable risk. Millions of women around the world are making important efforts to become more present and proactive in all aspects of social, economic, and cultural life. They stand together not as servants but as equal players who participate in world healing. Part of this important process is the rising awareness of ecological issues, which is a way of reconnecting with the energies of nature in a nurturing and respectful manner for the benefit of all mankind.

The rediscovery of the powers of Nature means also a renewed interest in traditional medicine systems and herbal lore: to work with plants and natural medicines is a woman's natural birthright and something women have always excelled at, naturally, instinctively, without the need for sophisticated machineries and laboratories. In the Amazon jungle there has never been a shortage of medicine women, even though when we think of shamans we have a tendency of imagining them as males. The reason women in shamanism are often a minority is due to their position in society, and their role as wives and mothers. In the case of Central and South American shamanistic practices, the taboos regarding sexuality have prevented many women from becoming plant medicine healers. A classic example of this phenomenon is the story of Maria Sabina, the famous Mexican curandera who, despite having a deep connection with Psilocybin mushrooms since early childhood, was not able to practice her medicine until much later in life when she became a widow and was no longer expected to fulfill any marital duties.[14]

Nowadays more and more women approach Ayahuasca and other natural medicines for the purpose of personal healing and spiritual guidance. Dissatisfaction with the ways of modern medicine and the rise of psychological and spiritual conflicts lead women to search for different approaches, often traditional and closer to Nature. Despite a more pronounced reluctance of women to engage with consciousness-altering substances, women benefit greatly from working with Ayahuasca and other Plant Teachers: not only do they get the healing they need, but this process also powerfully reconnects them to a realm they have been dispossessed of for far too long. The energy of Plant Teachers reawakens this ancient identity of women and Nature: it is an empowering experience that helps women heal centuries of alienation and distrust in themselves. At first some women perceive the energy of Ayahuasca

---

14   Estrada, Alvaro. Vida de Maria Sabina, la sabia de los hongos, Siglo XXI, 2007.

as too strong and too alien, like a poison rather than a medicine. This is not truly so, but is a consequence of centuries of estrangement from these energies. Persistence and trust in the medicine can allow them to heal this old wound and engage with the medicine without fear or concern. Eventually the medicine is seen for the great ally that it is: a healing energy that can reconnect each individual woman to her personal identity and sacred power.

Women are generally discouraged from drinking Ayahuasca during menstruation, not because they are necessarily believed to be impure, but because the effects of the medicine are greatly enhanced during this period. If a woman has problems and recurring pains connected with her menstruation cycle, these will be felt even more strongly under the effects of Ayahuasca.

Should a woman want to address issues concerning her reproductive system, then drinking Ayahuasca in smaller doses can be done, but only with previous agreement with the guide. This is not because of sexism of any kind, but the acknowledgement of the power of the Feminine manifesting radically during menstruation.

Embarking on a healing or spiritual journey with a male guide can be a challenging experience as one can unconsciously project all sorts of unresolved issues onto the guide – of course the same is valid in the case of men working with female guides and gay people working with a guide of the same sex. What is manifesting on the individual level is once again the conflictive relationship between male and female energies as experienced through collective and personal family history – what feels like a personal experience is really one colored by collective, transpersonal, and archetypal elements.

The abuses and power conflicts that have tainted our civilization are carried down from generation to generation until they are healed and integrated. Painful dynamics will keep repeating until their lessons are learned once and for all.

It is up to each one of us to stay aware of any judgment against our chosen guides, paying particular attention to gross generalizations (e.g., all men are such and such), or repeating patterns. When we refuse to give into such judgments and start examining ourselves as the source of these projections, then the people that seem to annoy or disappoint us beyond limit can be seen for the sacred mirrors and teachers they really are. Self-victimization has become a politically correct and all-too-recurrent attitude: women in particular could rightfully claim a long history of abuse with plenty of evidence at hand, but it's a disempowering dynamic that becomes a formidable obstacle blocking any real change and progress. And the time is ripe for women to regain their place in society, not as victims, but as responsible and powerful beings.

Without demonizing these natural occurrences, it will be stressed once again the necessity of not engaging in any romantic and sexual behavior while working with Ayahuasca, particularly in regards to the guide or shaman. This is particularly important for women to remember, lest they fall back into patterns of seduction or abuse. In any kind of healing therapy it is very easy to confuse the kind support received by the therapist as something other than what it is, and start fantasizing about a possible romantic relationship, which would distract one from the task at hand and most likely sabotage the whole process. Making sure we avoid the usual bag of tricks we employ to stay unaware and unconscious is a good way to regain awareness and evolve.

The spiritual path begins in earnest with the healing of our relationship with our mothers and fathers. This part of our personal healing process is perhaps the most important as it involves not only the parents but entire family trees, tribal groups, and collective issues such as gender discrimination and oppression that are centuries if not millennia old. The consequences of the relationship with our parents don't affect only our view and experience of gender, sexuality, and relation-ships, but also that of the Divine. As infants we regard our parents as gods, omnipotent and capable of everything we can't do but need for our survival. Our perception of the father figure is likely to color our idea of God, while the mother figure will affect our image and relationship to our bodies and the Earth. We each respond differently to these early psychic and psycho-logical imprints as each personal history is the result of various karmic elements: the soul finds the fitting envi-ronment for its evolution and the perfect classroom for learning what it came to this life to learn.

Self-acceptance and self-love pass through the critical eye of the needle of love and respect for one's parents, in which we are most closely mirrored whether we like it or not. The life lessons parents give their offspring are most important as they are received by the child with little if any resistance or boundary, and by the same token the wounds of childhood are the deepest and most difficult to face and heal. And so the healing journey with Ayahuasca begins, not by going down the rabbit hole but often by going back into our mother's womb, into our parents' mothers' wombs, all the way to the source of human Life, in order to heal all the relations and wounds we encounter along the way. This is a very profound process for women today because it allows them to let go of old inherited dynamics that prevent them from becoming the lovers, wives, and mothers they aspire to be.

Maternity has often been kind of taken for granted by men, but these days we are called to reconsider this, and take better care of the mothers of our children for upon them rests the future of our species. The sooner we face these issues and release the weight of the past, the sooner we will be able to stop perpetuating the conflict between men and women and the resulting damage that afflicts humanity.

There is no mother without a father, and there is no Feminine without the Masculine: the same issues that haunt women afflict men just as well. We have acted for centuries believing in wars that create winners and losers, but in reality everybody suffers equally because of conflict. The ultimate unity and identity of all human beings, beyond their gender, sexual orientation, race, culture, or creed, is a reality that needs to be honored and taken into consideration now more than ever.

In the Greek dramatic dialogue, The Symposium,[15] the philosopher Plato wrote about what is perhaps the last myth in Western civilization regarding the origins of the human race. This myth tells of a human race

---

15   Plato, Symposium, Oxford University Press, USA; 2009.

made of people with two heads, eight limbs, and both male and female sexual organs. They were a powerful race that became arrogant, to the point that the god Zeus decided to weaken them by cutting them in two, which caused people to start looking for their missing half. The power of love is that of reuniting two halves of the same being, thus achieving wholeness. To become one with the other is the wish of the soul, of all souls. Human happiness is achieved by returning to that state of primordial unity.

In our times this myth has come to mean the necessity for people to reconcile and reunite the Masculine and the Feminine within themselves, thus regaining and embodying the consciousness of divine androgyny. Balancing these two energies and fully respecting their expressions wherever they manifest is the task ahead for all human beings. Transcendence of all dualities and emergence into a peaceful way of life starts by reconciling these two energies inside our hearts.

PERU

As stated earlier, the increased interest of shamanism in general and plant medicine in particular has turned Peru into a major destination for spiritual seekers of all kinds, to the point that Peruvian consulates abroad explicitly advertise Ayahuasca healing as a way of bringing visitors to this country.

In 2004 I was very fortunate to join a group of people lead by a wise and dedicated man who had been coming here for many years and was very familiar with the ins and outs of this land. My first visit was so positive that I ended up moving here the following year. Over the years I have visited a handful of retreat centers in the Peruvian Amazon and worked with various healers, all of who turned out to be very knowledgeable, generous, and caring. Unfortunately not everyone who comes here succeeds in receiving from their visit what they had hoped for. Perhaps this is because of their unrealistic expectations, or because of the challenges of being in a foreign country and culture, often with little or no ability to speak the local language.

Speaking of unrealistic expectations, I feel it's important to warn people about certain indigenous people who promise healing of any kind of physical ailments and incurable diseases, the nature of which they may have never even heard of. It is a fact that jungle medicine has proven effective against many diseases, but it is also true that in the case of ailments that are relatively new or unknown to Amazonian people, then often no remedies against such ailments have yet been developed here.

As a developing country with an emerging economy but also a lot of poverty and often a mediocre infrastructure, Peru confronts us with a reality that is difficult for many Westerners to accept and respect as is. Even though we come here as guests, it is hard to resist criticism regarding things like inadequate services, garbage management, and a seemingly chaotic atmosphere.

For many visitors the challenging lesson of surrender begins unexpectedly as soon as they arrive at the Lima airport with flight delays, missed connections, and lost luggage. Our need for control is rapidly frustrated and the only options at our disposal are to either go with the flow or suffer. In this regard, having plenty of time at our disposal and a loose schedule that can be easily rearranged is often the best way to visit this country.

I had never before traveled with an organized group but I didn't regret it at all as it helped me get my bearings without the stress of having to figure out everything by myself, such as finding a way out of Pucallpa at the end of our visit to the jungle when we discovered that the only airline serving that town at the time had been shut down by the police a few days earlier.

When it comes to working with Ayahuasca here the choices are endless: healing centers that offer retreats, places we may have learnt about through friends, the internet or the medias, serendipitous meetings, or an adventurous search in unknown places. To our own disadvantage we sometimes come here with some assumptions that may be perfectly valid in our own countries but are out of place here. One of them is the belief that plant medicine should be free of charge. This unfortunately does not take into consideration the fact that for many curanderos their work is not only their calling but also an important source of revenue in regions where money and resources are scarce.

Monetary transactions can be a touchy subject and one should be as clear as possible about the price of any service, from taxi rides to healing ceremonies, before making any commitments. Still, it is not uncommon for a Peruvian person to ask for more money than was agreed upon after they have provided their services. Sometimes the price hike is reasonable, and sometimes it isn't – a mixture of flexibility and steadfastness is the best attitude.

Because of the scarce economic resources that keep many Peruvians at a basic sustenance level, I highly discourage people from expecting monetary refunds: in most cases the money that was given has already been spent and the expectation of a refund can be cause of hostility and resentment.

For me spending money in this country, which relies a lot on tourism, including spiritual and medical tourism, is a way to practice Ayni – reciprocity. This is why I am happy to conduct my healing work exclusively in Peru: even though it would be more ecologically sound for me to travel alone and conduct ceremonies abroad instead of everyone who wants to drink Ayahuasca with me to have to take a long airplane flight, I feel that by having people visit me and spend money here this whole country receives a fair return for all the gifts we receive from Ayahuasca.

Another phenomenon that comes hand in hand with scarcity here is the high incidence of envy, which I believe to be a more insidious plight than poverty or corruption. The collective belief in a finite amount of resources is cause of resentment and envy by those who have less and feel that those who have more have necessarily taken something from them. As the whole of humanity is presently dealing with scarcity issues and their repercussions on a social as well as individual level, I feel that Peru offers to us all a very powerful mirror of some interesting, but limiting beliefs. Competitiveness is rampant among shamans along with greed, envy, and jealousy, all themes that at first seemed strange to me within the context of drinking Ayahuasca. Yet, with time I realized that I was not immune from such feelings and living here has helped me tremendously in finally taking an honest look at them.

It is easy for us Westerners to fall prey to the idea of the "noble savage," untouched by modernity, materialism, and greed. The reality is that natives are just as fascinated by money and gadgets as we are and will pursue them as assiduously as we do. Expecting these people to keep living exactly the way they have for centuries while we storm into their villages with powerboats, laptops, and digital cameras is a bit naïve – I don't see why they shouldn't be allowed to indulge in the same things as we do.

The temporary abandonment of traditional ways and their rediscovery once we find out that the pursuit of material things isn't going to bring us everlasting happiness seems to be a cycle that has already begun here and there in Peru and it will play itself out in its own time. In the meantime the race toward modernity seems unstoppable and we can only wish that new lifestyles will not completely erase the traditional way but integrate with them.

The arrival of foreign visitors in remote areas can have radical and traumatic effects on native populations just as it did here 500 years ago, but we can apply the lessons learned from past mistakes and minimize the damage this time around. I feel that the presence of Westerners here is not necessarily a calamity but an opportunity to heal together the wounds of the Spanish Conquest, which are still open after so much time.

Peruvians are for the most part very happy to see us visit their country and appreciate their traditions and cultures: this is a huge step after centuries of Western cultural and religious imperialism, and is helping them reconnect with their old ways, including their shamanic and healing practices. This is particularly true in regards to Ayahuasca: the global attention that this medicine has been receiving in the last few years has sparked among locals a renewed interest in traditional shamanism. Whereas before most people would prefer to move to larger settlements where they could enjoy some of the comforts and entertainments of modern life instead of having to spend months of solitude in the jungle in order to learn plant medicine, the prospect of being able to make a living as a curandero is motivating the new generations to keep their healing and spiritual traditions alive for the benefit of their communities and all of mankind.

AYAHUASCA AND THE FUTURE

The resurgence and rising popularity in the use of plant teachers all over the world, from Peyote and San Pedro cactus to Iboga and Ayahuasca, correspond to a global need to reconnect to a traditional wisdom that modern science and thinking had relegated to quackery and superstition. The return to these medicines actually fills a void left in the human spirit by the materialistic viewpoint of rationalism, so much so that the ceremonial use of Plant Teachers is rapidly expanding beyond their original cultural environment while keeping the same power to heal and guide.

Despite the development of modern technology, the issues of humanity have not changed, and among them are not only material survival and the pursuit of comfort, but also the need to explore and find answers to the perennial questions such as inescapable death or the deeper meaning of Life. In the confusion of modern times we have gone back to traditional wisdoms with the hope of finding meaning in our lives so that we might deal with the troubles of a highly technological and globalized society. To me personally this is not a romantic return to a mythical past but the rediscovery of tried-and-true tools and rituals that may help us deal with the present and the unknowns of the future. This means not only reconnecting with ancient traditions, but also adapting them in the best possible way. The evolution of the use of Ayahuasca is one such example. The adaptation of the use of this medicine is a natural one: Ayahuasca has remained a valuable tool for humanity, whether it is to help hunters find their prey in the jungle or support others in healing or discovering new technologies, such as the HTML computer code, in places far away from the Amazon basin.

We are aware that the survival and evolution of humanity entails the ability to develop a greater degree of clarity, access the deeper truths within ourselves, and have the courage to manifest and embody such truths. The spirit of Ayahuasca generously offers the guidance and healing we need in these times. Ayahuasca does not expect anything from us in return and will keep sharing her gifts provided we go to her respectfully and don't turn a deaf hear to her teachings.

The message of the plant is, "let go," and it's only by letting go of deeply ingrained fears, conflicts, and limiting beliefs that we can achieve peace in our hearts and in the world. We live in extraordinary times, and at the same time we are plagued by increasingly big problems but blessed with the necessary tools to solve them. Throughout history we have developed not only technologies for production, traveling, and communication, but also for healing the body and the spirit. Ayahuasca is but one of the many medicines available today. It has been with us since time immemorial and will keep spreading its counsel and sharing its wisdom among those who honor it until the end of time.

The journey ahead may be filled with challenges but we are not walking it alone. We are supported in our quest for harmony and balance by the whole of Creation, of which we have always been part. Nature is not only a reservoir of bankable materials, but also an intimate mirror in which our creative power and deep intelligence are reflected. Beyond the greed that may cloud all judgment lie the real treasures of our planet: not the material goods that can make one financially rich, but the spiritual teachers, and among them Plant Teachers, and allies that can help us ultimately become better human beings, more kind, compassionate, and loving.

EMBRACE OF THE
SERPENT

As we come more and more in contact with native people and cultures, we can't escape the
fact that the consequences of such meetings go both
ways. It is often enough a positive exchange but, if I
may say so, we Westerners can seldom resist the temptation of wanting to "improve upon the lives of the natives" in always well intentioned but usually damaging
ways.

Unfortunately one such area is the Western
intervention into traditional plant medicine shamanism:
we come to Ayahuasca or San Pedro with our
arrogance, impatience, and westerly ways, imposing
our belief that more and faster is always better. We
go to these medicines thinking that what we are
ingesting is a compound of miracle molecules when in
actuality what we are drinking is neither just DMT (the
visionary molecule of Ayahuasca) nor mescaline (the
psychoactive ingredient of San Pedro), but a whole

plant with a much more complex vibration than the sum of a few molecular compounds, the wisdom of the psychic space of the place where they are from, and the wisdom gathered through time by all the people who have engaged with such vibrations.

To think of these medicines as inert psychoactive substances is wildly reductive. I think this is what Maria Sabina, the Mexican curandera who worked with Psilocybin mushrooms, referred to when she said that her medicine had lost its power when Westerners started ingesting it: by seeing these plants as simple chemicals we reduce them to something much smaller, and therefore less powerful, than they really are. Luckily the foreigners who approach these ancestral medicines with such small-mindedness seem to be able to expand their appreciation after ingesting them.

Personally, the bigger cause for concern lies in changes traditional plant medicine keeps incurring in order to satisfy the appetite of money-bearing foreigners. Nowadays programs are offered that are so intense and excessive by any traditional standards and common sense that I doubt the native people offering them would ever encourage any of their family members to follow them.

In order to make money, natives and foreigners alike are willing to speed up a process that has time and patience as its most important requirement in order to unfold positively. Nature has a slow rhythm and, no matter how quick the transformation plant medicine is able to offer, we still need to offer this process the necessary time for it to unfold beneficially.

In the case of Ayahuasca, I usually don't recommend more than ten ceremonies over a period of a month, followed by at least two weeks of integration afterwards, and this with as little activity between ceremonies as possible, adequate nourishment, and plenty of rest.

Plant medicine as I understand it is as much about the expansion of consciousness as it is about being able to ground that expansion and wisdom into the body and our everyday life. As I've witnessed in individuals who have abused this medicine with excessive frequency and lack of proper integration, the result is not clarity but confusion, often leading to paranoia or a dangerously delusional state.

To underestimate the power of Ayahuasca and engage with it indiscriminately does bear consequences. To approach it with caution and respect each and every time, and under the proper guidance if someone is not experienced or not mature enough (psychologically and mentally) to do it by oneself, cannot be recommended highly enough. In the end it is always better and easier to prevent the damages of possible abuse than mend them afterwards.

In 2016 what I consider to be a most important Columbian movie, *Embrace Of The Serpent*,[16] was released on DVD. I quickly ordered a copy and was impressed not only by the story and the cinematography, but also by the poignancy and relevance of the themes explored in it.

---

16   Guerra, Ciro. *Embrace Of The Serpent*, DVD, 2016, Brooklyn, Oscilloscope Pictures.

The movie is about two historical yet fictionalized Westerners, Theodor Martius, a German ethnographer from the 1800's, and Richard Evans Schultes, who is considered by many the father of modern ethnobotany. Both characters explore the Amazon forest for their academic studies but they are both also looking for something they need: the former is dying and is looking for a cure, the latter has been engaged by the U.S. government to find ways to grow rubber trees during WWII after Malaysia and its rubber plantations were taken over by the Japanese. These two characters exemplify what motivates to this day most foreigners when they go to the Amazon: the search for healing and natural resources. In both cases their (and our) needs are pursued with a classic Western attitude imbued with disrespect, greed, impatience, and ignorance.

The jungle is a very powerful yet delicate environment and ecosystem where all beings, plant, human, and animal alike, thrive thanks to their harmonious symbiosis. The movie depicts the many mistakes these two Westerners make as they enter this unknown environment because of their lack of respect, humility, and wisdom.

The first lesson these two men need to learn in order to continue their journeys is that they are travelling in the jungle with too much baggage, too much stuff. That baggage is an example of our Western attachment to things and objects, and is a good metaphor of our attachment to the physical and the material, which often ends up slowing down our spiritual journey. The other aspect of such baggage is the mental and cultural baggage we bring with ourselves wherever we go, among which is our belief that we know better than and are intellectually superior to others. Both men are repeatedly invited to let go of such baggage, their technologies, and their mindset, so that they can connect and learn from the jungle directly and without mental constructs that, as valid as they may be back at home, are now rather useless. In order to learn any student is required to be humble and have an open mind, but this movie shows us that even these two men of science are not in the Amazon to learn but to *get something* out of it, and how the pursuit of our appetites and needs makes us blind and disrespectful of everything else, even to the point of endangering our own lives.

People of European descent have held this dangerous and aggressive attitude towards foreign lands and people since modern Western colonialism began in the 16th century. Even though colonialism as such is a thing of the past, it has been replaced by so-called free trade agreements where Western countries still have the upper hand. The most insidious aspect of colonialism, which is about objectifying and exploiting people and natural resources, is unfortunately still quite alive today. It is so pervasive that it even colors our attitude towards native cultures, religions, and spirituality.

In *Embrace Of The Serpent* neither of our two white characters can dream: they are so in their minds that the vast realms of the unconscious, of archetypes, and myth are totally unavailable to them: despite their technological superiority and money they are perceived as hungry ghosts, barely alive, and asleep. They roam the jungle like hungry ghosts looking for something to assuage their hunger, spiritual and physical, but they do so without respecting the ancestral laws of the jungle over and over again, stubbornly holding on to the very cultural and psychological predicament that is the cause of their hunger. And in their stubbornness they bring death and devastation wherever they go, spreading their spiritual disease instead of healing it. In the end Theodor Martius dies in the jungle and Richard Evans Schultes is forced to let go of his agenda and expectations altogether in order to receive the real gift that the jungle has to offer him and his people.

In the movie it is said that sacred plants (and all plants are sacred in the jungle) are in the Amazonian tradition not to be cultivated, meaning that they are not to be exploited and traded in the way we Westerners think; and that the way to connect with them and receive from them is a matter not of money or convenience, but of being spiritually and psychologically ready. That spiritual and psychological maturity will ensure that those gifts end up not being traded and benefitted from for selfish empowerment, but shared for the benefit of all.

So what are the important lessons for us all that history and this movie offer to us? The most important lesson for me is about letting go, whenever we engage with another culture and are visiting another place, of our Western materialism and utilitarianism, which make us perceive everything as a commodity to own rather than honor.

In regards to ancestral plant medicines such as Ayahuasca and San Pedro, what I have seen happening is an increasing attitude of manipulation and distortion of the use and purpose of these medicines by foreigners both here in South America and elsewhere. A symptom of such manipulation and distortion is clear in the lassitude towards dietary and behavioral restrictions, and in the mixing and matching of medicines and processes in order to speed up the process or avoid certain aspects thereof. An example of this is the increased popularity among foreigners of Rapé, an Amazonian sacred snuff used as a ceremonial cleanser and medicine: foreigners all over the world can be seen nowadays using this medicine outside of ceremony and administering it to themselves and others without the guidance of someone truly knowledgeable, and they often use it in plant medicine ceremonies in order to speed up the purging process so as to avoid the unpleasantness of nausea. The first case speaks of our arrogance in insisting upon using medicines and spiritual tools without the proper training and often distorting their use; the second scenario speaks of our unwillingness to honor ancestral ways that have been developed over millennia and of our determination to use these medicines in any way we wish in order to avoid whatever aspect of the healing process we deem unpleasant or time-consuming. Once again we exercise a kind of cultural colonialism that is not only disrespectful but also potentially very dangerous, and in so doing we often fail to receive the very healing we say we seek.

I believe in constant evolution and I am not against change and progress, but I honestly don't see how people without extensive knowledge and experience with these medicines can beneficially change ancestral methodologies from one day to the next. This is not in my opinion evolution but manipulation, and a manipulation that distorts something very precious and valuable as it is. If we don't refrain from our colonialist and consumerist attitude, we risk destroying yet another important part of our human cultural heritage, not to mention the diluting and lessening of power of ancestral medicines. The best way to avoid such negative repercussions is to resist the urge to improve upon what other cultures and people have been doing for so long in the name of effectiveness and progress, and as if we really knew any better, and approach them instead with respect, humility, and patience. Plant medicine is not for everybody, meaning also that if we are not willing to honor this process and its ways, then it would be better for our own sake and health not to engage in it at all.

Moving through and beyond our Western paradigm of ego-centered consumerism and appropriation is in itself part of the healing that we seek as individuals and as a collective, and in my opinion the only way to receive the real gifts that these ancestral medicines and cultures have to offer us as modern people, just like it happened to our fictionalized Richard Evans Schultes at the end of *Embrace Of The Serpent*.

SUSTAINING A CULTURE OF SAFETY AND AWARENESS IN PLANT MEDICINE

The increased popularity and use of Ayahuasca and other plant medicines worldwide, despite their illegal status in many countries, entails a necessary raise of awareness towards safety. I say "necessary" because the rising numbers of people engaging in this process makes what used to be an under-the-radar phenomenon a matter of public health and safety. In some countries plant medicines are tolerated despite their illegal status, but that tolerance may quickly disappear and be replaced with repression should people die or end up in psychiatric wards in significant numbers.

The illegality of these medicines makes them also unregulated and not subject to any quality control whatsoever, which in my opinion means that it is up to all of us to exercise discernment whenever we engage with them, at home and abroad, if we wish to avoid any future repressive governmental reaction. I feel this is a wonderful opportunity for us all to take responsibility for our own lives and health, and I believe it is possible to sustain a culture of safety in regards to plant medicines.

Taking personal responsibility each and every time we engage in this process will have the immediate and welcome result of lessening the amount of useless gossip and judging in medicine circles: whenever we take responsibility for our choice of ceremonies and plant medicine people, then any complaint and judgment appear in all their ludicrousness. The awareness that we get exactly what we sign up for and that what we sign up for is not necessarily what we want but what we need, opens the space for a true ownership of our judgments and projections, thus furthering the healing process.

I have seen and heard over the years how the deflecting of responsibility, by expecting some sorts of unspoken and unwritten quality standard to be present whenever and wherever we chose to engage in this process, or through some naïve assumption that plant medicine circles and their members are somehow exempt from human imperfections and flaws, has not really helped improve the quality of the plant medicine world in any way. Perhaps then it is time to let go of such expectations and assumptions of others, and take greater care whenever we choose a ceremony or retreat.

For this purpose I offer here a series of questions, one for yourself and the other for the prospective ceremony leader or host, that may help you better assess whether this or that experience meets your needs for safety and support. The biggest challenge around making the right choice for ourselves is that too often we are quick to dismiss our gut feelings and just go ahead and pursue what we want despite some clear signs that point in the opposite direction. Over the years I have become increasingly discerning about where, when, and with whom I engage in this process: as limiting of choices as my discernment may be, I am very happy to exercise such discernment each and every time, even at the cost of foregoing some very interesting and alluring experiences. I exercise the same care that I would in the case of choosing a dentist or surgeon, and why wouldn't I since this is about my physical, emotional, mental, and spiritual health? And whenever I am in doubt I simply say no and stay home. Getting out of our comfort zone is one thing, and foolish risk-taking is another thing altogether.

These questionnaires are based on a list of questions created by Michael Costuros of Entrepreneurs Awakening[17] when he started bringing groups of entrepreneurs to work with me and plant medicines here in Peru. Michael's focus on quality and safety for the people who join his retreats is exemplary but not the norm in the world of plant medicine. The creation of such questionnaires has been his way to make prospective participants more aware and more actively engaged in making sure that they make the best choice for

_____

17 http://www.EntrepreneursAwakening.com

themselves. If we approach this process with greater responsibility, discernment, clarity, and honesty, we can continue to sustain a level of health and safety in our medicine circles that will benefit not only ourselves and our communities, but the collective consciousness as well.

QUESTIONS FOR ONESELF BEFORE SIGNING UP FOR A CEREMONY OR RETREAT

- What is my general state of health? Do I feel physically fit enough to experience a possibly challenging healing experience?

- What are the medications and supplements, prescription and non-prescription alike, that I have been taking recently? Are any of them contraindicated in the case of ingesting Ayahuasca?

- Have I had any surgeries in the previous six months that may require some more healing before I engage with plant medicines again?

- What has been my consumption of recreational drugs, alcohol, and caffeine (including chocolate) recently? Am I willing to abstain from all of them before, during and after the medicine process as required by my host?

- Do I have a history of depression, bouts of paranoia, or mental breakdowns that indicate that I am not psychologically ready to engage in this process? Am I open to discuss any such trouble with the host before they agree to allow my participation?

- In the case of a single ceremony, am I willing and can I set aside a minimum of 12 hours before AND after the ceremony without social, personal, and professional commitments of any kind so that I can mentally and emotionally prepare for the ceremony and have a minimum of time afterwards to begin integrating it with ease?

- Am I willing to be off-line and off the phone for the entire duration of the ceremony and possibly a few hours before and after?

- What are the reasons for my wish to join this ceremony or retreat? (You may want to take some time and even pen and paper to list all the reasons and then see whether these are good enough to sign up or not. For instance you may find that one important reason for joining a ceremony is that you are a little bored or lonely. If that were the case you may want to invite your friends over for dinner instead.)

- What do I hope to receive from this experience? (If you realize that what you are seeking can be easily found in other ways, then I would forego the medicine approach.)

- What is my support network for after the ceremony/retreat?

- In the case of joining a group I have joined in the past, is there any ongoing dissatisfaction about such group? Are there any unmet needs that are important for me to talk about with the group, host, or ceremony leader before I join them again? Are there any projections that would benefit from some exploration before signing up?

- Do I feel that such community is still the best place for me to engage in this process, or is it time for me to find another?

QUESTIONS FOR THE HOST AND/OR THE CEREMONY LEADER BEFORE SIGNING UP FOR A CEREMONY OR RETREAT

- What is the size of the ceremony or retreat group? (I believe that if someone is looking for healing and is in need of support, no ceremony or retreat with more than 20 participants can realistically provide such level of support, and would therefore refrain from joining them.)

- What are the facilities and services offered? (These include overnight lodging, bathrooms, and transportation.)

- What is the monetary or energetic exchange required?

- Who are the people leading and assisting the ceremonies? How long have they been offering ceremonies? What has been their training? What tradition did they apprentice in and for how long, and what tradition are they following now? Do they have a teacher they have learnt from and who has given them the permission to lead public ceremonies with this medicine?

- Where does the medicine offered come from? Has the medicine been harvested in sustainable ways? How does the community where the medicine comes from actually benefit from this exchange?

- In the case of people leading the ceremonies who speak a different language than ours, will there be a sober interpreter at all times during the facilitators' visit?

- When is the medicine person arriving at the site of the ceremony? And how long are they staying after the closing of the ceremony? (I feel it is most important to be able to talk to the medicine person before and after the ceremony if one feels the need. Ideally the medicine person would be available until noon the day after the ceremony in order to address whatever question or need.)

- What kind of preparatory information and guidance is provided before the ceremonies?

- What kind of support in regards to integration after the ceremonies is offered?

- What is the screening process on the part of the host like? Does the host meet personally with each participant?

- What kinds of songs are sung during ceremony?

- What plants are in the Ayahuasca brew? (Despite its appeal, I would discourage anybody unfamiliar with Datura from drinking any Ayahuasca containing this powerful and equally dangerous plant.)

- What kind of support and healing is provided to every participant during the ceremony or retreat?

ENDINGS

EPILOGUE

Aldous Huxley was fond of quoting William Blake's words "Gratitude is Heaven itself,"[18] and I think of no better way to end this book than by thanking everybody who has supported me in writing this book.

First of all I want to thank the Spirit of Ayahuasca for guiding and giving me the strength to write this book – my only hope is to have listened and followed her advice well.

My deepest thanks to Ken S. for introducing me to this amazing medicine and for bringing me to the Amazon jungle for the first time in 2004, to Don Francisco Montes Shuña of Sachamama Ethnobotanical Garden in Iquitos for being such a gifted, generous, and wise teacher in the realm of Amazonian plant medicine and spirituality, and all the spiritual Teachers who keep guiding me on my path.

Thank you to all the teachers I have had the honor to work with and learn from here in Peru: Jose' and Rony in Pucallpa, Leoncio Garcia, Kevin Furnas, Fredy "Puma" Quispe Singona, and Lesley Myburgh. Thank you to Harry Chavez in Lima for his beautiful and inspiring art, to Erin McAuley for her poem, and to Electra and Daniel Reeves for their precious help in bringing this book to completion.

Thank you to Diane Dunn and everybody at Paz Y Luz Healing Center in Pisac for their continuing support of my work, and for their friendship.

---

18 Huxley, Aldous. Moksha, Park Street Press, 1977.

Thank you to my parents, Luisa and Ignacio, and my dear friends Jeff Rose and Pascal Bacon for their love, generosity of heart, and unconditional support.

Thank you to Jesse Krieger and everybody at Lifestyle Entrepreneurs Press for publishing this book.

Thank you to all the people who have supported my work all these years, and to all the people who have sat in ceremony and shared their beautiful energies with me: you have been the sweetest of medicines, thank you!

And finally thanks to you, dear reader, for reading this book – may this be the beginning of wonderful new adventures towards the Light.

Pisac, Peru. April 7, 2014

BIBLIOGRAPHY

Bourbeau, Lise. Heal your wounds and find your true self, Saint-Jerome, Editions E.T.C., 2001. **Print.**

Burroughs, William and Ginsberg, Allen. The Yagé Letters Redux, San Francisco, City Lights Books, 2006. **Print.**

Estrada, Alvaro. Vida de Maria Sabina, la sabia de los hongos, Mexico City, Siglo XXI, 2007. **Print.**

Huxley, Aldous. Moksha, Rochester, Park Street Press, 1977. **Print.**

Lamb, Bruce F. Wizard of the Upper Amazon: the story of Manuel Cordova-Rios, Berkeley, North Atlantic Books, 1993. **Print.**

Lamb, Bruce F. Rio Tigre and beyond: the Amazon Jungle Medicine of Manuel Cordova-Rios, Berkeley, North Atlantic Books, 1993. **Print.**

Narby, Jeremy. The Cosmic Serpent, New York, Penguin/Putnam, 1998. **Print.**

Plato, Symposium, New York, Oxford University Press, USA; 2009.

Rätsch, Christian. The Encyclopedia of Psychoactive Plants, Rochester, Park Street Press, 2005. **Print.**

Williamson, Marianne. A Return To Love. New York, HarperOne, 1992. **Print.**

Supplements to A Course in Miracles, published by Foundation for Inner Peace, New York, Viking Penguin, 1996. **Print.**

RECOMMENDED READING

Calvo, César. The Three Halves of Ino Moxo, Rochester, Inner Traditions, 1995. **Print.**

Davis, Wade. One River, New York, Touchstone, 1997. **Print.**

Schultes, Richard Evans and Raffaut, Robert F. Vine of The Soul, Santa Fe, Synergetic Press, 1992. **Print.**

Grof, Stanislav. LSD: Doorway to the Numinous, Rochester, Park Street Press, 1975. **Print.**

Huxley, Aldous. The Doors of Perception, New York, HarperCollins Publishers Inc., 1954. **Print.**

McKenna, Terence. The Archaic Revival, New York, HarperSanFrancisco, 1991. **Print.**

McKenna, Terence. Food of The Gods, New York, Bantam Books, 1992. **Print.**

Naranjo, Claudio. The Healing Journey, New York, Pantheon Books, 1973. **Print.**

Watts, Alan. The Joyous Cosmology, New York, Pantheon Books, 1970. **Print.**

ABOUT THE AUTHOR AND THE ARTIST

Javier Regueiro is a Spanish national born and raised in Lugano, Switzerland. He is a certified Massage Therapist, Rebirther, and Avatar Master.

He moved to Peru in 2004 to study Amazonian plant medicine and shamanism, and has apprenticed with various teachers in the Iquitos and Pucallpa areas. He has undergone several months of shamanic diets, learning the use and healing properties of plant teachers such as Ayahuasca, Tobacco, and Datura among others, and has become a full-time plant medicine person since.

His commitment is to make Ayahuasca and San Pedro available to all people who feel called to use these medicines for personal healing, spiritual guidance and the evolution of consciousness.

He lives in Pisac, Peru, where he has created the Ayaruna Center and conducts his healing work with traditional Peruvian plant medicines.

He can be contacted through the website, www.Ayaruna.com.

Harry Universidad Catolica of Peru, Harry Chavez (Lima, 1978) has studied Korean art and culture at Dankook University, South Korea. His work integrates the wisdom and iconography of ancient cultures, with particular emphasis on the Peruvian Andean and Amazonian worldview. Making a powerful synthesis of this knowledge with a unique technique, he proposes a lively, contemporary mythology.

He has had solo exhibitions in Lima, Iquitos and Cusco and participated in various group exhibitions in Peru, Argentina, Chile, Bolivia, and Spain.

He can be contacted at https://www.facebook.com/harry.chavez.

CPSIA information can be obtained
at www.ICGtesting.com
Printed in the USA
LVHW02s0718020818
585538LV00005B/7/P